HOW TO HAVE
AN
OBEDIENT DOG

By the same author

The Right Way to Keep Dogs

Also available from Elliot Right Way Books

How To Have A Well-Mannered Dog
The Right Way to Keep Cats

Uniform with this book

Front cover
Photograph courtesy of Ardea London Ltd,
35 Brodrick Road, Wandsworth Common,
London SW17 7DX.

HOW TO HAVE AN OBEDIENT DOG

Jackie Marriott

RIGHT WAY

DEDICATION

To the first two dogs I owned during my adult life, Simon and Rupert, two little 'terrors' who set me on the dog training road. Also, to my beloved Brumas, my first Bernese, who taught me, and gave me, so much.

THANKS

To my husband and fellow Dog Trainer, Vic, whose help and assistance has, as usual, been invaluable, and to Sandy Enzerink BVMS MRCVS for checking the medical details and for her expertise in caring for my animals' health.

CONTENTS

LIST OF ILLUSTRATIONS

INTRODUCTION

Why Train Dogs?

The relationship between man and dog goes back many centuries, when man discovered that dogs were more efficient hunters than himself. Over a period of time he domesticated them to help him hunt, in return providing shelter and a share of the kill. It was a partnership from which both benefited. This, combined with the dog's social needs, i.e. a pack formation requiring a leader (man), led to the forming of bonds which have lasted to the present day.

Over the centuries, dogs have been used for a variety of tasks apart from hunting. These include retrieving game, herding sheep and other livestock, guard duties, guiding blind people and, more recently, as ears for the deaf. Dogs that were good at certain jobs were used for breeding and as a result the distinctive breeds developed.

Nowadays, large numbers of dogs are kept purely as pets and do not have any specific duties, other than being a companion. Those dogs which were developed for working, however, need to use and develop their basic instincts. Training can either encourage this, or, where the instincts are undesirable, channel them into activities which are acceptable in society. Training is essential for the big, strong breeds, but is also beneficial for smaller breeds, to improve nervousness or subdue aggression.

Well cared for, healthy dogs, are not carriers of disease nor are all dog lovers cranky or eccentric. However, because of the enormous amount of adverse criticism over recent years, owners need to train their dogs to be more socially acceptable.

Nobody likes dirty streets or dogs roaming in packs in urban areas. Nobody likes to hear about sheep being worried by dogs, or dogs left out to fend for themselves. Dogs, unlike people, have no morals; they do not know and abide by our codes of behaviour unless trained and supervised by a responsible owner. We cannot blame the errant dog, any more than we could blame a cat for following its natural instincts and killing a mouse, or a fox for killing a rabbit.

The methods used for training are basically very simple. We make as much use as possible of the natural instincts. As previously mentioned, dogs are pack animals in the wild, one dog being pack leader. This is usually the most powerful and intelligent dog. He may be challenged from time to time by subordinates and if a stronger dog wins the battle, the leader is replaced. In training dogs, we take over the role of pack leader, by inspiring respect, showing the dog we are superior to him, but also as soon as he complies with our wishes, he will receive affection and comfort.

1

PSYCHE OUT YOUR DOG!

Dog Logic
In an ideal world, before anyone acquired a dog, they would attend classes in canine psychology, study genetics, examine every breed for positive and negative traits and read all about the potential pitfalls of dog ownership. However, this is not an ideal world and the reasons why people get a dog are as varied as the breeds themselves.

The very best time to start training is whilst the dog is still a puppy, before he has a chance to learn any bad habits. Some of you reading this book may well be in that situation and you are the ones who should have the easiest job of all. Others may have had their dog for a few weeks or months and the problems have only just started to appear. Others still may have given a home to a 'rescue' dog and perhaps, because of its previous home, the dog may have been allowed to develop many unacceptable habits, or have all kinds of phobias, both real and imaginary.

For all of you, the methods described in this book will enable you to have a happy, well adjusted and well controlled dog.

Before you start, it is as well to understand just how your dog 'works'. Much as you love him, you must accept that he is not blessed with human emotions, that he is an animal and a pack animal at that. By 'pack', I mean that in his original and wild state, he was one of a group, with a leader, number two, number three, etc., in descending order. Where in the pack he stood depended on his character, physical strength and qualities of leadership.

Man has since domesticated the dog, but the very strong basic pack instinct remains and once the dog enters your family, he will look upon it as his 'pack'. It is entirely up to you who emerges as the leader – you, or the dog! If it is the dog, your family life could end up with the dog ruling everything, making your life and that of the rest of the family a misery. Perhaps you are already in that situation? If you are, or don't want that situation to develop, you must start now, setting yourself up as number one in the pack, with the rest of the family behind you and the dog at the bottom. I assure you that once he recognises you as 'boss' and knows his place in the pack order, he will be a much happier animal.

As in all packs, there will be times when he will attempt to challenge your leadership and each challenge must be met in the same way – you are boss!

Priorities

Your dog has three basic priorities. Starting at the top, they are *food, affection* and *comfort*. Food being his most important, he will rarely, if ever, leave it for either of the other two. Comfort being the least important, he will happily leave lying down for a cuddle from you. He will quickly leave a cuddle if food is offered. You can demonstrate this with your own dog, to prove the point. Using these priorities correctly will be invaluable when it comes to training your dog. (See *Reward*, opposite.)

Correction

Although I have used the word correction here, there are rarely, if ever, any occasions when you should need to physically correct your dog. Hitting a dog with anything, be it your hand, a stick, a lead or a rolled-up newspaper is counter-productive. A 'hands-off' approach avoids having a confrontation which may result in your dog biting you, either through fear or, as he sees it, self preservation. Avoiding the use of physical correction is not backing down, it is simply making use of the conditioning which the dog has already received from his natural mother.

As a new-born pup in the litter with his natural mother, he was taught from the moment of his birth what pleased his mum and what didn't. When he was naughty, she would grumble and growl, sometimes quite ferociously. Sometimes she would even nip him. Conversely, when he was being good, she would 'stroke' him with her tongue and 'cuddle' him, being very soft and gentle. She would allow him to play-fight with her, but never let him get the upper hand, always putting him in his place when the time was right.

If you get the chance, go and watch a bitch with her puppies. She can teach you more about dog behaviour than almost anyone else. Now, I'm not suggesting that you start biting your dog, but what you can do is to utilise that first basic training he learned from his Mum, and adapt it to fit. When your dog is displaying behaviour which is not accept-able to you, as his 'replacement' parent, use your voice in a grumbly tone. Don't touch him at all – to be touched is pleasant for the dog, and he sees it as being rewarded. Sometimes completely ignoring the dog is enough of a correc-tion. He wants your attention and praise, and to be denied both will make him understand that you are not pleased. He will have a remembered association with the conditioning he received at the 'paws' of his Mum, and will understand that his actions have not pleased you. What he will then want to do is earn your pleasure, rather than displeasure, so after any altercation, tell him to do something which you *know* he can do, so that you can reward him for pleasing you. (See also *Mouthing and Play-Biting*, page 98.)

Reward

Many owners find it difficult to show genuine pleasure to their dog. Often they feel a pat on the head and a gruff 'good dog' is all that is needed. Worse still are the owners who think the dog ought to 'know' when they are pleased, on the assumption that the dog understands language. There is still a school of thought that thinks that if you show real affection towards the dog when you are pleased, it will affect your position as pack leader, and is somehow demeaning! Perhaps that attitude stems from the traditional 'British stiff upper lip'. They feel that displays of affection will be interpreted by the dog as a sign of weakness. They may also feel that they will lose control if they allow the dog to play and 'let off steam'. Nothing could be further from the truth!

Just imagine for a moment how you would feel if you had completed an exceptional job of work and no-one bothered to say 'well done', or if they did say 'well done', they said it begrudgingly. It would hardly inspire you to try as hard next time. Consider how you would feel if you spent all day preparing a dinner party, and not one of the guests said 'thank you'. Would you invite them back? I think not! Suppose pay-day came around at work and suddenly there was no salary. Would you continue working? Think of rewarding the dog in terms of his wages and signs of appreciation for a job well done. Reward every attempt on his part to 'get it right'.

To make the training as crystal clear as possible to your dog, you will need to use his natural priorities, as previously mentioned. Initially you can use food in the form of *small* tit-bits as a primary inducement and reward, together with verbal and physical affection, *and lots of it*, each and every time your dog gets your message right. Gradually you will be able to reduce the use of tit-bits, as long as you have ALWAYS backed up the tit-bit with physical and verbal reward. *Show* the dog you are delighted with him by giving him big, enthusiastic cuddles. Stroke and touch him lovingly. *Tell* the dog you are pleased with him, either in a soft and gentle voice or slightly louder if the conditions or the action warrants. Don't rely solely on the use of tit-bits. Dogs aren't daft – if they only get rewarded with food, come the day when you've forgotten to put any in your pocket and you'll find that you suddenly have a deaf dog! When you are using tit-bits, make sure they are suitable dog-type food (*not* biscuits or chocolate bought for your consumption!), and only give *tiny* pieces, otherwise you could end up with a very fat dog! As a rough guide, use a tit-bit the size of a cat biscuit – in fact cat biscuits make good tit-bits for dogs! Or, you could use part of the dog's daily food ration as tit-bits, setting aside a portion each day which he will earn, by pleasing you, rather than have it in his dinner bowl. Obviously, if you are feeding your dog 'wet' food as opposed to dry food, that could get a bit messy, so perhaps the cat biscuits would be better in those instances!

Boundaries

One of the earliest lessons your dog has to learn when he enters your family is where his boundaries are. By this, I mean what you are going to allow him to get away with. If you don't want him on the furniture, for example, then don't let him start. If he has already requisitioned a chair and you would rather he hadn't, then insist he removes himself, refusing to accept any show of aggression and praising him like mad when you succeed.

Don't make the mistake of treating him as you would a naughty child. There is an important difference between the two – a child has the ability to reason, a dog hasn't. You can explain to a naughty child why he is receiving punishment and he will understand. Dogs do not understand language and do not have the ability to reason, so any punishment or correction must be given *as he commits* the offence, otherwise he will not understand what the punishment is for.

I can almost hear you say 'oh, but he knows when he's done wrong, he looks sad and runs away'. No doubt he does know that you're angry, but I promise you that unless you actually caught him in the act, he does not and cannot know what has provoked your anger.

Let me give you an example. Suppose you have left the dog on his own and whilst you were out, he has chewed a big hole in the settee. You return home and your dog, thrilled to see you, comes rushing up to welcome you. You spot the ruined settee. With a face like thunder and a voice to match, you shout and scream at him, perhaps even hitting him. What have you taught him? You've taught him that when you come home, the best course of action for him to take is to run and keep well out of the way, as you're so cross when you come home. He has no way of knowing that his act of demolition, maybe done more than an hour before you returned, is the reason for your temper. How can he? He's forgotten all about it, the second he stopped chewing.

OK so what *should* you have done? In you come, dog rushes up to greet you. Having spotted the ruined settee, ignore it, cuddle your dog and let him welcome you home. Next, go up to the settee, *showing no sign of anger whatsoever*. Now encourage him to start chewing the settee! Sounds daft! No, because as he puts his teeth to it, that's when you correct him. Show him at that instant that what he's doing is wrong. He will immediately associate your anger with the action he is doing, i.e. chewing the settee. Apply this to anything he does which you dislike, i.e. digging holes in the garden, foraging in the rubbish bin, chewing your shoes etc., and he will instantly learn what is allowed and what isn't.

All the dog wants is to know where he stands and to be loved by you. All the time he is being good, love him to pieces. He will only want to do those things which get a favourable response from you and will not want to repeat any action which incurs your displeasure.

2

INFORMAL TRAINING

By informal training, I mean all those things which you want to teach your dog *not* to do, as opposed to formal training, which is teaching him things which you want him to do. Informal training can start from the moment he enters your house.

Possessiveness with Food

Having said earlier that food is his most important priority, an early and vital part of your establishing yourself as the leader is by showing him that he can only have his food at your discretion and command. Give him his dinner, let him eat for a few seconds, then take his bowl away from him. Use an appropriate sound each time you do so, such as **leave** or **stop**, and keep the bowl for a few seconds. Provided he did not show any sign of aggression as you removed the bowl, tell him 'good boy', give it back and allow him to continue eating. Repeat this two or three times during each meal for a few days, then once or twice a week for a few weeks.

Some dogs are never possessive with food, but you may find that if your dog came from a large litter, the way he obtained his share was by threatening his brothers and sisters. If such action achieved the desired result, i.e. getting more food, he may well try that with you. If you don't sort this out very early on, this possessiveness will transfer to other things, such as bones, toys, furniture and so on, perhaps even to members of the family.

To stop him being aggressive with his food, don't give him possession of it! In other words, feed him by hand for at least a couple of weeks. Prepare his food in the bowl as usual, but don't put the bowl on the floor for him. Simply feed him a handful at a time. The presence of the bowl of food on the floor almost instinctively makes him want to guard it, so if he is not put in the position of needing to guard, he will not bite! Feeding him by hand also helps if your dog is dominant in other areas. It makes him completely reliant on you for the most important thing in his life i.e. food, and will therefore reinforce your position of pack leader, as he is only getting the food from you, not from a bowl. You can also use the period of hand feeding to reinforce your control further, by making him perform some minor order from you for some of the food. Get him to sit first before one handful, or to lie down for the next, and so on. Obviously, don't make him run about for the food – that could lead to digestive upsets, or worse. Sedentary acts, however, will not do him any harm.

You will find that after a couple of weeks of this regime, his general demeanour over possessions will alter. You can then try giving him his food in a bowl again, and, provided there is positively no sign of aggression, continue to feed normally.

For dogs that are food possessive, do not give them bones or toys, as they will attempt to guard these in the same way. Once the food possession has been sorted out, you can try introducing a toy, but make sure the dog understands that it is *your* toy, which he is allowed to play with only with you, and when *you* decide that the game is to end, *you* always end up with the toy. (See also *Mouthing and Play-Biting*, page 98.)

Coming when Called – Early Training

Although this will be covered more fully in Chapter 3, you can start to formulate this exercise before ever putting a collar and lead on your dog. Food being the dog's first priority, use it to 'condition' him to come when called.

Make sure he is in another part of the house whilst you

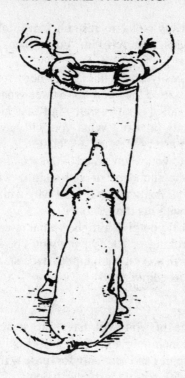

Fig. 1. Dinner is served!

prepare his dinner. When you are ready, have the bowl in your hands, holding it at chest height. Signal your dog to come, by calling his name and giving him the sound **come**, said with a very pleasant tone. His sense of smell will have already 'told' him what is going on and he will no doubt come rushing to you. As he arrives at your feet, don't allow him to jump up for the bowl, but tell him to **sit**. Keep the bowl at chest height and do not give it to him yet. He will probably sit more than willingly; in fact at this stage he would probably walk across the ceiling if you told him to, such is his desire for food! Once he has sat, tell him to **wait** and place the bowl on the floor in front of him. Any attempt to get the bowl must be stopped; if necessary hold his collar to restrain him. Make him wait at least five seconds, then tell him 'go on then, good boy' and allow him to eat his food.

Now, quite easily and without any need for harsh correction, you have started the build-up to three separate exercises – coming when called – sit – wait – all of which you will be teaching formally later on. What you will have succeeded in doing is to start a very pleasant association in your dog's mind with returning to you when called to the sound of **come**, sitting when told to the sound of **sit** and waiting when told to the sound of **wait**, all being rewarded not only with a verbal sound from you, but with his dinner too!

Make sure that you give him the verbal reward clearly, plus some gentle stroking, as later on you won't be using his dinner bowl as a reward, so you want him to understand that praise is verbal as well as edible!

House Training

Although some of you will have progressed beyond this problem, I am including a section on it, firstly for those who have young puppies and secondly for those who are experiencing problems with a previously clean dog.

There are many different methods for teaching a dog to be clean and most people have their own 'pet' theory. Like everything you want your dog to learn, you can teach him to be clean on command, by giving him a sound to go with the action! If you are having difficulties with house training, I suggest you start again from scratch and try my methods.

The old wives' tale of rubbing the dog's nose in it is not only most unpleasant for all concerned and completely illogical, but more importantly it doesn't work. Likewise, it is no good 'putting' your dog outside in the garden and hoping he will relieve himself. He may well do so, but he will not be learning anything.

Dogs need to go to the toilet at certain regular times, such as on waking, after a meal, after playing. Make sure that at all these times you immediately *take* him into the garden, staying out there with him, even if it is cold, wet and dark. As soon as he starts to relieve himself, give him a command to go with his action. I use 'hurry up', but you can use any words you like, provided you keep them short.

Remember too, that you will eventually be giving him this same command when he is outside, with other people around, so do choose something sensible! Reward him profusely as he finishes, lots of 'good dog, clever dog', etc.

If he always receives that praise when he relieves himself outside, he will quickly learn to associate the action with the reward. Any accidents indoors should be ignored. You may be able to stop him just before he squats, in which case quickly but *calmly* take him outside. Don't panic him, or he will forget what his original intention was.

With young puppies, you should take them outside at least once an hour to begin with. Again, with young puppies, you can start training them to paper if you prefer, although it does take a little longer to get them clean this way. Cover an area of the floor with the newspaper and take the puppy to it at all the relevant times, giving the same commands and praise as you will when he is outside. Over a few days, gradually reduce the area of paper, moving it slowly towards the back door. Move it progressively over the back doorstep and outside.

Make a point of putting the puppy on his lead sometimes when you take him out to be clean in the garden. He has to learn to relieve himself whilst being confined on a lead and some dogs get quite confused if previously they have only ever been running free when they want to relieve themselves. If you don't put them on the lead occasionally, it can take a long time to get the idea through to them that sometimes they have to remain on the lead and still go to the toilet.

GETTING CLEAN THROUGHOUT THE NIGHT. Getting the dog clean through the day is relatively easy, but the long period during the night can be a problem.

This could be for a variety of reasons. Sometimes, the young dog has simply not yet learnt to control himself and here you can try using the newspapers on the floor just for night-time use. It could be that he is 'asking' to go out and has been unable to attract your attention. If this is the case, it may be worth setting your alarm clock a couple of times during the night, just for a week or two, so that you can let him out. Admittedly this will mean a broken night's sleep for you, but if the end justifies the means, so be it. Perhaps he has learned that if he stands by the back door, he is let into the garden, but of course at night-time nobody can see him as everyone's in bed. (See page 31 for advice on indoor kennels.)

It may be worth investing in a little DIY here, which can help solve the problem. Get a thin flat piece of hardboard and buy an ordinary battery-operated doorbell, complete with wire. Fix up the bell outside your bedroom door, running the wire to the back door, to floor level. Attach the bell push towards the edge of the board and connect up the wire. Place the board, bell push side down, on the floor by the back door, if possible under the floor covering. When you put pressure on the board, the bell should ring. When your dog next goes to stand by the back door, asking to go out, he will stand on the board and hey presto! He will have operated the bell, alerting you that he wants to go outside. I have used this with several of my puppies, to great effect.

Sometimes it may just be a matter of altering his feeding times. If he is normally fed his last meal of the day around 6 p.m. his natural bodily functions will decree that he will want to relieve himself at about 3 a.m. Try either bringing his last meal forward, or leaving it until much later. Also, to ensure that his bladder is empty before he goes to bed, pick up the water bowl at 5 p.m. Obviously, if he has been playing energetically, allow access to the water for a short while to satisfy his thirst, then remove it again.

ONLY GOING TO THE TOILET IN THEIR GARDEN. There are some dogs who, having grasped the idea of going to the toilet in the garden, seem to think that is the *only* place they can go. You take them out for a walk, but they 'hang on' until they return home. Maturity usually tends to solve this particular snag, but in the meantime it can be quite a problem, especially if you are taking the dog out for the day, or going away on holiday. You must persevere with the training, encouraging him all the time he is outside, giving him the command he has learnt in the garden.

If necessary, stop him going into the garden at all for a few days. On every occasion when he normally wants to go to the toilet, put him on his lead and take him out to the park or wherever, giving him his command and, eventually, nature should take over! This may be time-consuming but it will pay dividends in the end.

In view of the enormous amount of publicity which has been given to the problem of dogs fouling public areas, it can sometimes be a positive advantage if your dog prefers his own back garden! Do try and be a thoughtful dog owner when you are out exercising your dog. No-one, dog owner or non-dog owner, likes stepping in dog excreta, so always take a few plastic bags with you so that you can clear up after your dog. Plastic bags are not cumbersome and are very simple to use. Just place your hand inside the bag, scoop up the 'deposit', turn the bag inside out using your other hand, seal it and place it in the nearest litter bin. Your hand will not come into contact with anything unpleasant and your dog will not be causing any offence by leaving little 'presents' behind him!

ACCIDENTS CAUSED BY EXCITEMENT. This seems to be more common with young animals and usually affects bitches more than males. Usually the dog doesn't want or intend to be dirty, but gets so excited that he simply cannot help himself. First of all, DO NOT PUNISH THE DOG, you will only make matters worse, as the dog will become so nervous of your reaction that he will relieve himself through fear. To try and overcome the situation, be very calm when you first greet your dog – not cool, but controlled, and immediately go through to the garden with the dog, where you can greet him properly and any 'accident' will not matter.

Usually they grow out of this problem, but if it persists, it may be something physical and a trip to the vet may be necessary.

HABITUALLY DIRTY DOGS. With some dogs it becomes a habit to urinate and defecate wherever they choose. It may be that they have never been properly house trained, or because they have a very strong territorial instinct and feel the need to mark out their territory.

In the first case, where the dog has simply been allowed to become dirty, you must go right back to the basic training, as you would for a young puppy. If he is a 'territory marker', he may be urinating on the furniture, especially in a strange house. Obviously, if you can catch him 'in the act', a quick correction may save the day – and the sofa! It doesn't seem to make any difference even if the dog has just relieved himself outside – the instinct to leave his mark is so strong. If the problem only occurs when you take him to strange houses, the only answer may be not to take the dog in.

If the problem is happening in the dog's own home, then try moving the furniture, as often dogs tend to do it in the same spot and by putting a piece of furniture on that spot, you may break the habit. There are products you can buy which have a smell and taste repugnant to the dog. Sprayed over the relevant area this may help to stop the dog dirtying that spot.

There is a theory that with male dogs who urinate indoors, having them castrated can be the answer. It does work sometimes, but castration is *not* the answer to every training problem, as some people tend to think. It most certainly should not be contemplated until the dog is completely mature and then only after discussing it thoroughly with your vet.

There is now available a course of injections which can simulate temporarily the result of castration and is worth considering before you have your dog operated on. If the injections work, there is a good chance that the castration will too, but if they don't work, the chances of castration working are remote. In Chapter 5, page 115, I go into the advantages and disadvantages of both castrating male dogs and spaying the females, so please read as much as possible about the likely outcome of such operations, before you take such a step.

BACKWARD STEPS. It is quite common for dogs who have previously 'got the idea' of being clean to revert to being dirty again, usually when they are around four-to-five months old. This generally coincides with them starting to teethe and is only a passing phase. Understanding and patience are required and a few days' repetition of initial house training will usually sort the problem out.

Likewise, some bitches become dirty indoors just before they start their season. It is basically because their hormones are 'having a sort out' and is only temporary, so do be patient. Emotional upset within the family, moving house, or indeed any change in the normal routine can get the dog's 'wires' crossed temporarily. This especially applies to 'rescue' dogs, who may have undergone quite an emotional trauma and are having difficulty adjusting to a new home and new routine. Do be really patient, treat the dog as you would a young puppy and the problem will soon be solved.

Routine

Because any upset in routine can cause possible problems with house training, it is important that you establish early on a regular routine for your dog. All the important things in his life should happen in a regular pattern, such as eating, walking and sleeping, allowing his head and his body to get into a 'system'. Imagine the effect on his stomach if you fed him at 8 a.m. on one day and at 2 p.m. the next. His stomach would soon get very upset, as would his sleeping and toilet routine.

The same thing happens if there is no regularity in his life and no consistency over what he is and is not allowed to do. He can only adapt into the human way of life if he has a regular timetable, i.e. feeding, sleeping, exercise, playing, being left, etc. Even though it is not ideal for you to leave your dog all day whilst you go to work, he can adjust to long periods of being alone – although of course you will have to make sure that the time he does spend with you is as full and interesting as possible.

As well as the routine of the household, you should get him into a regular routine of being brushed and 'looked at'. Examining your dog may sound strange, but if you get him used to his ears being checked, his teeth, eyes, feet, etc., all being held and examined, it will make your job, and that of the vet, much easier when the dog is unwell and in need of attention. It is very difficult, for example, to bandage up a cut paw when the dog won't let you near his feet!

Get used to the look and feel of him when he is healthy, so that you will quickly be able to spot when something is wrong. For those of you who have a female dog, make sure you know what her intimate parts look like, so that you will be able to see the difference when she starts her season. If you don't know how to tell when she is in season, by the time you do notice, it may be too late – she may already be pregnant!

Leaving the Dog Alone

At some stage, your dog is going to be left at home alone, either whilst you go to the shops or perhaps whilst you go to work, etc. If you first teach him that being left is part of his normal routine, he will accept the situation without either being destructive or howling the place down!

To start conditioning the dog to periods of being left alone, you must first be able to leave him in one room, whilst you are in another. Start by putting him in a room on his own with the door shut, for just a couple of minutes, two or three times a day. Don't be tempted to go back in if he cries or barks. Ignore it! Only go back in when he is quiet, and always be pleasant when you go and let him out. That way he will learn that barking and/or whining gets no reaction, but being quiet does. Slowly build up until he will be left happily for up to an hour on his own shut away from you. Then you can progress to actually going out, knowing that he can cope with being left.

When you decide that you are now going to go out and leave him, first make sure that where you will be leaving him is safe and secure. Perhaps a safe toy left with him will deter him from chewing or playing with other items which could harm him, or your bank balance! (See Howling and Chewing.) Start teaching him a set of sounds that he will learn to associate with you always saying before you go out, which he will learn means that he is remaining behind, but that you *are* coming back. I usually say 'just going over the road, won't be long' every time I leave my dogs. They now associate those sounds with me going, then a period of being left alone, then me coming back, as I have done every time after I have given them those sounds.

Having decided on what you're going to say, say it and leave the house. Stand outside the door, very quietly. As when you were conditioning him to be left in one part of the house when you were in another, don't go back if he cries or whines. When he has been quiet for a few minutes, go back indoors and greet him happily.

The dog will learn from this that barking and whining gets no reaction from you, so it serves no purpose and he will stop. On the other hand, when he is quiet, you eventually come back to him and greet him pleasantly.

Slowly, over a period of several weeks, gradually increase the length of time you leave him, so that you can build up to leaving him for as long as your routine requires. Please don't leave him for too long on his own though – I consider three to four hours is the maximum a dog should be left alone – even then not until he is mature and not on a regular basis. Dogs are naturally gregarious; they like people's company and if they are left alone for long periods they can become either depressed or destructive, or both.

HOWLING AND CHEWING. Sometimes the silence of an empty house can distress the dog and may start him howling or barking. Sometimes, because of the silence, dogs can hear noises outside more easily, thereby provoking them into barking. Try leaving the radio on when you go out, as the sound of human voices may soothe the distressed dog and mask the external sounds for the barking dog. Some dogs learn to be very destructive when they are left alone and young puppies, particularly, like to chew, especially when they are losing their baby teeth. In this instance, leave them something they *can* chew which is not going to matter. I have found that a pile of empty cardboard boxes, the sort you can get from the supermarket, provide a dog with endless amusement, as they can demolish them beautifully! Of course, you must remove any staples or wire first.

By leaving the boxes for him to chew, you are getting two distinct benefits. Firstly, he is not damaging the furniture or the carpets and all you have to clear up when you return are pieces of cardboard. Secondly, you will not inadvertently be teaching him to chew anything precious, as you would if you gave him an old slipper or shoe to play with. If you do actually give him an old shoe to demolish, you can hardly be surprised when he chews up your best pair – how is he supposed to know the difference between old ones and new ones?

For puppies who are teething, I have found that an old saucepan or frying pan comes in useful – and no, not for hitting him with! When he's teething, he wants something cold and hard with which he can ease his painful gums, so you can see that such an article is ideal. Obviously, make sure there are no sharp edges or loose screws on which he could harm himself and don't use the non-stick variety, as this could poison him. One word of warning here – if he tries to carry it around in his mouth, watch out for your shins, as a clout from a metal pan really hurts – and I speak from very painful experience!

Incorrect diet may also cause a dog to chew, especially if there is a lack of fibre in the dog's daily rations. Door frames and wooden furniture then become a replacement for the missing elements of the dog's daily needs. Check with your vet if you think this could be relevant to your dog, and he or she will be able to give you some diet suggestions.

Lack of exercise and mental stimulation can also create the need for the dog to relieve his boredom and stimulate his brain by chewing and destroying. What you have to realise is that his actions are *not* done out of spite. The act of chewing is self-rewarding, either to ease the aching gums, chewing something that smells of you, or even employing the killing instinct by chewing your settee! Most chewing (and destruction) is usually done whilst you are out. Imagine how shocked and confused the dog becomes when you return home. He has been indulging in a self-rewarding and pacifying activity, with no thought of upsetting you. Then you come in and are very angry. This in turn can lead to chewing through anxiety, and so the whole procedure becomes a vicious circle.

INDOOR KENNELS. An indoor kennel, with one special item for the dog to chew, may be an answer if the chewing cannot be overcome.

Dogs are natural denning animals – indeed they often create their own dens around your home without you realising it. Under a table or chair, in the corner of a room – all these areas can become a den for the dog.

An indoor kennel is basically a secure, comfortable area, big enough for the dog to turn around, stretch and stand. You may be able to convert an area already chosen by the dog and simply block it off with wire mesh. Alternatively, you can make a complete wire mesh kennel, or purchase one from a pet shop.

Start getting the dog used to the kennel by feeding him in there, without shutting the door on him. Leave it open during the day, to encourage him to go in there of his own accord. Put a comfortable bed area in one end, and a bowl of water at the opposite end. Prevent him from having access to other 'home-made' dens of his choice by blocking or barricading them off. Whenever you see him go into the den you have chosen, give him a cuddle and a tit-bit whilst he is inside.

After a few days, start shutting him in the kennel for a few minutes at a time, whilst you are still in the house. Put a favourite toy in there with him, and always reward him for being in there. Once he is happy to be left inside, you can start to leave him for longer periods of time, whilst you go out. Because he can't be doing any damage whilst in there, you will always be able to praise him when you return home.

Finally *DO NOT MAKE THE DEN A PLACE OF PUNISHMENT*. Never make the mistake of either sending or forcibly taking him to his kennel when you are cross. The 'den' must always be associated with comfort, food and safety. Make sure too that before he is left in the den, he has had access to the garden so that he can go to the toilet. He will get very distressed if he has to soil the den.

Dogs who Steal

It is quite natural for a dog to take things in his mouth – after all, he doesn't have hands! Unfortunately, it is often the owners who inadvertently teach their dogs to steal. A fairly typical reaction to seeing your dog wandering around with your best pair of socks in his mouth, is to chase after him and shout at him to leave them. He runs away and it turns firstly into a game and secondly into a way of challenging your authority and getting you to lose your temper. This all culminates in him stealing at every opportunity.

What you *should* do is to encourage him to bring whatever he has in his mouth to you, by praising him and telling him what a clever dog he is, saying 'good boy, come and bring it here'. When he does come up, all pleased with himself, reward him and tell him to **give**, holding your hands level with his mouth and taking the article as he opens his mouth. As you are going to be ever so nice when he brings it to you, he will enjoy your reaction so much that he will not want to run away. He may even end up actively seeking things out to bring to you.

You will probably end up with the sofa piled high with socks, clothes, shoes, slippers, shopping bags, etc., but at least they will not have been hidden or destroyed. He will have learned a valuable lesson in what pleases you, plus you will have the added bonus of laying down the groundwork for the retrieve exercise. Retrieving is not necessary for the average pet to learn, but if you want to do obedience competitively later on, you will have already done some basic training towards it.

Jumping up

Why do dogs jump up? Usually because they are pleased to see you and jumping up gets them closer to you, especially your face. Think about your reaction when the dog jumps. You probably touch him with your hands to push him off. Or to 'get it over with', you stroke him, say 'hello' and are generally pleasant.

Either way, as far as he is concerned his action of jumping has received a favourable response from you, i.e. you have touched him and spoken to him. So he will repeat the action which gave him that response – he will jump up again.

To stop him jumping up, or even wanting to, you need to turn his action into an unrewarding one, whereas up to now it has been rewarding – you have touched him to get him off, albeit that you see it as pushing him off. You have also been talking to him; again you have seen it as telling him off, he sees it as getting attention.

If your dog is still a puppy, as he goes to jump at you, turn your back, fold your arms and IGNORE him. When he has stopped attempting to jump at you, be it after a few seconds or even after several minutes, tell him to **sit**, and immediately he does, go down to his level and reward him. Once he realises that by sitting, he gets the attention he wants, he will not feel any need to jump at you. Try coming in and going out several times in the course of a few minutes – after being ignored a couple of times, you will find that he will sit very willingly, eventually without being told. Ask each member of the family to adopt the same procedure, then set up some visitors to do the same thing.

Provided you never forget to reward him for NOT jumping, he will stop this anti-social behaviour.

If you have an older dog who is still jumping up, you need to adopt a different approach. Although part of the reason why the dog jumps up is the same, there is also an element of dominance-related behaviour in adult dogs. Height equals status to a dog, and if he can obtain that status at the same time as touching you, the more important he feels. Ignoring the dog is not enough, so as he goes to jump at you, glare at him coldly and say in a loud voice '**GET OFF**', and then turn your back and ignore him. Again, once he has stopped attempting to jump, tell him to sit and reward him – you will be rewarding him for sitting, remember, *not* for not jumping up. If he tries to jump up at your back, take a step or two away from him. As with the puppies, if his actions (jumping up) do not provoke the *re*action he wants, he will cease.

Please do not use the word **down** for this exercise – **down** is later going to mean something else, and you do not want to confuse the dog, or give him a chance to misunderstand.

Finally, it will help if you teach the dog formally to say hello to visitors by always sitting first, being rewarded with a tit-bit from the visitor. That way you will again reinforce to the dog that the way to get what he wants is to sit. If you use the words 'say hello' on every occasion when a visitor arrives, you will soon find that he will sit immediately when a visitor appears.

Barking

The dog which barks unnecessarily is a pain to live with and agony to live next door to! Some dogs bark because their guarding instinct is very strong and they feel it necessary to alert you to every little noise. Some bark because they are nervous and the sound of their own barking gives them confidence. Some bark because they like the reaction it provokes in you and some bark simply because they haven't been taught not to. It is quite normal for a dog to bark if someone comes to the door or if he hears a strange noise during the night. Continuing to bark after an acceptable time is what you want to deter.

In most cases, the way to stop a dog barking is to teach him to bark on command! This may sound very strange, but it does work. At the same time as teaching him to bark, you are also teaching him when *not* to bark.

For the dog to learn this exercise, you need to enlist the help of a friend, so that you can set up the situation. You should be sitting relaxing, then your helper, at a pre-arranged time, should come to the door and ring the bell. Your dog will then naturally bark and as he does so, give him the command **speak**. Allow him to bark for five seconds, then command him **quiet**, giving him lots of fuss when he does. Don't attempt to answer the door until the dog is silent. Then go to the door, open it, speak to your friend on the doorstep, as you would a casual caller, then close the door.

Go back and sit down again and after an interval of about ten minutes, repeat the whole · process again. Alternate between talking to your friend on the doorstep and inviting him in, to simulate what would sometimes happen, i.e. someone coming to the door, then being invited into the house.

Try to repeat this over a few days, building up the association with the dog that he is allowed to bark for just a few seconds when that doorbell rings, but he must stop when you say so, the door never being opened until he has stopped barking. You are also getting him to associate the sound of your command **speak** with his barking.

Why must the door *never* be opened until he is silent? If you allow him to continue to bark whilst you open the door, he will associate that it is his action of barking which gets the door open, resulting in future problems. If he is the type of dog who imagines there is someone at the door and barks often unnecessarily, the only way you will get him to be quiet is to go and open it. You may even end up in a situation of the dog training you – every time he wants attention, he will bark to provoke you into getting up to answer the door to an imaginary caller.

Having taught him to bark on the command **speak**, you will then be able to get him to bark if ever you feel in a threatening situation – when you're out for a walk, perhaps, and are approached by a suspicious character, or if you should hear a strange noise in the middle of the night. You can also apply the same training if your dog barks every time the telephone rings. Arrange for a friend to telephone you and don't answer until the dog is quiet. On these occasions though, don't practise by giving him the **speak** command, as you don't want him barking every time the phone rings. Simply correct him for barking unnecessarily at the telephone.

DOGS WHO BARK BECAUSE THEY LIKE THE REACTION IT PROVOKES: Sometimes it is your action in response to the dog barking which can actually make the situation worse. In an attempt to shut the dog up quickly, you tend to rush to answer the door or the telephone and in the process get the dog even more excited. If you think you may be guilty of this, then deliberately do not answer the door, etc., having previously arranged with a friend either to telephone or ring your doorbell. If you show no sign of agitation with the ringing noise, you will take the excitement out of the situation.

You may have fallen into the trap of shouting at the dog each time he barks – or even taken to chasing after him to get him to be quiet. As far as he is concerned, the whole thing turns into a game, at the same time he has learned how to provoke you and get you to lose your temper, thus challenging your authority as pack leader.

He may be the type of dog who simply stands in the garden, head thrown back, barking like crazy and waiting for some reaction from you. If you recognise this situation, indulge in what I call 'negative' training. As it is your reaction which excites and stimulates him, you are going to show no reaction whatsoever. It isn't easy to ignore a barking dog, but you need to give an Oscar-winning performance of complete indifference! Don't speak to him, don't look at him, read the newspaper, pretend to be asleep, show no reaction *at all*. The dog will then probably become curious as to your lack of interest and will come over to you enquiringly. When he does, give him a calm, gentle pat, tell him 'good dog', etc., and carry on reading. As far as he is concerned, it's no fun if he can't get you to react, so he will shut up.

After a few minutes of silence, make a point of going over to him and fuss and play with him. You are thereby conditioning the dog that noise gets no reaction from you, but when he is silent he gets the attention he wants.

THE NERVOUS, HYSTERICAL BARKER. If you have the type of dog who rushes out into the garden, barking at unseen terrors, or simply rushes out barking because he likes the sound of his own voice, shock tactics can sometimes work.

Have ready a plastic jug filled with cold water. When he starts his ear-splitting routine, sidle up to him very casually and throw the water over his head. Don't speak as you do it, but praise him like mad the second he stops. Better still, if you can arrange to 'bomb' him with the water from an upstairs window, or from an unobserved position, without him realising where the water has come from, it can be far more effective. Once again, he will have received a most unpleasant reaction to his barking, which should prove quite a deterrent in the future.

This method can also be applied if you have a dog who barks whilst travelling in the car. Substitute for the jug a water pistol or plant spray. When the barking starts, aim the jet of the spray between his eyes, again saying nothing as you do it, but praising like mad when he stops. It is obviously much safer if someone else is driving the car at the time!

Car Travel and Travel Sickness

Many dogs develop a fear of car travel and become sick during the journey. Unfortunately we as dog owners inadvertently contribute towards this.

Usually the very first experience a dog has with a car is when you collect him from the place where he was bred. The trauma of leaving his mum, brothers and sisters, plus the people he has become used to, is compounded by being put into a moving machine, possibly for several hours. The car thus becomes an upsetting place, associated with being taken away from his first family.

Then, he settles in with you and more than likely his very next trip in the car is to the vet for a check-up and his first inoculations, again compounding his opinion that cars are most unpleasant places to be, this time associated with having an injection. The car has turned into a monster and his dislike of it increases. Fortunately, most dogs do grow out of this phobia as they mature, but some retain their hatred.

There are various things which you can do to help him overcome this fear and reinstate the car as a place of pleasure. Use his highest priority, food, and start to give him one of his daily meals in the car, whilst it is parked outside your home. His love of food should overcome any reluctance to enter the car, coupled with lots of encouraging sounds from you.

When you have done this for a few days, set aside half an hour, when you can take your dog to the car and sit in there with him, again whilst the car is stationary. Turn the radio on, talk calmly and lovingly to him all the time. When you've done this a few times, start the engine, letting it run for a few minutes, still talking all the time to the dog. Don't try and rush any stage.

When he seems calm being in the car while it is stationary, yet with the engine running, plan a short trip, either to the park (assuming he has had all his inoculations), or to visit someone whom the dog is fond of. Slowly, build up the association that nice things happen when he is in the car, gradually increasing the time spent in the car and the distance travelled.

If he is prone to being sick, make sure that he travels with an empty stomach. For the very nervous dog, the type who tries to charge around in the car, restrain him by attaching his lead to a strong bracket inside the car, putting him in the down position. Leave him enough room so that he can turn his head, but not so much that he can sit up and move about.

Dogs who will not remain still are not only very dangerous in a car, but the tearing about only succeeds in winding them up further. In very extreme cases you can obtain tranquillisers from the vet, but try not to rely on these permanently.

Strange Sights and Sounds
As soon as you bring a new puppy into your home, start accustoming him to as many different sights and sounds as possible. This applies equally to older dogs as well, which you have given a home to, as you have no way of knowing what might frighten them. Get them used to all the usual domestic noises, such as the washing machine, vacuum cleaner, hair dryer, etc. Deal with any show of fear as it arises, being very calm, patient and loving. As soon as the dog has had all his inoculations, make a point of taking him along roads which have heavy traffic, accustom him to pedestrian crossings, level crossings, etc. Take him across pedestrian bridges and under pedestrian subways. If he shows apprehension at any of these things, don't avoid them, but make a point of taking him to them regularly. For example, if he is showing fear of heavy traffic, take the time to stand on the pavement with him – obviously well back from the edge of the road – talk calmly to him all the time, stroke him and if necessary, give him the odd tit-bit. Don't baby him, or try and avoid taking him past any of his 'terrors'. You will only make matters worse. If you are too sympathetic, it will only convince him that there really is something to be frightened of. He needs to get his confidence from you, so adopt a gentle but chivvying attitude, be kind, lots of fuss, but don't try to protect him.

If your puppy is still small, don't be tempted to pick him up. Apart from not curing his fear, you could be setting up a situation when he will ask to be carried – easy enough when he only weighs a few pounds, but a full grown labrador or similar is not so easy to pick up! Likewise, if you have a small dog, which is easy to carry, please don't. However tiny they may be, they are *dogs*, and as such should be treated like dogs, not children.

Make a point of taking the dog to crowded, noisy places. An ideal venue to socialise your dog is the local pub. The combination of crowds of people, juke boxes and fruit machines will all help to make him completely bomb-proof. Of course, another advantage of taking him to the pub is that it gives you a perfect excuse for 'popping down to the local'! Don't forget to take the dog though!

Getting your Dog used to Children

If you have children in your family, make sure they under-stand that the dog is *not* a toy. Most dogs brought up with children are incredibly tolerant towards them and will put up with treatment that they would never accept from an adult. Provide the dog with a place of safety to which he can retreat when he's had enough. If all the children understand that when the dog takes himself off to his basket, for example, he is to be left alone, the dog will willingly put up with all kinds of things, as he knows he can escape whenever he wishes. Don't let the children torment or degrade the dog, however tolerant he may be. They must be taught to respect the dog, in the same way that the dog must respect them.

If you haven't any children at home, get the dog used to other people's children as soon as possible. Dogs who are nervous or aggressive towards children can be quite a handi-cap. Children can be quite unkind to dogs, prodding and poking them, shouting and rushing about, so make sure that the children to whom you introduce your dog have themselves been properly trained! At the first meeting, use food as an inducement and have the child give the dog a tit-bit, thereby giving a pleasant association to the dog in connection with children.

Finally, however well behaved your dog is around children, it is most unwise to leave a dog alone with young children. Anything could happen, from the children letting the dog out onto the road, to their provoking the dog so much that he ends up biting them. The dog cannot speak and his only answer to cruel treatment, however unintentional it may be, is to use his teeth.

Young babies especially should never be left alone with any dog. As far as the dog is concerned, babies make funny noises and smell very interesting, arousing his basic natural instincts and curiosity, which could have disastrous consequences. Having said that, don't immediately get rid of the dog if a new baby comes along. Just be sensible and vigilant and the two of them will happily co-exist.

Dog Training Clubs

As soon as your puppy is old enough, join a dog training club. More and more clubs are coming around to the opinion that the earlier a puppy starts his training the better and will let you join as soon as the puppy has had all his inoculations. As well as the advantage of getting help with training problems, it is an excellent way of socialising your dog with people and other dogs.

Clubs usually advertise in the local paper, library and vets' waiting rooms. Go along and watch a couple of times before joining, to assess whether it is the right club for you. Are the instructors continually telling the members to praise their dogs? Are they explaining *why* the dogs do certain things, as well as how to deal with each problem? Are the dogs working happily, tails wagging? If so, these are all good indications that the instruction and training is on the right lines. Talk to the other members, find out about the social aspect of belonging to the club. Use your common sense and you will soon work out whether it's a good club.

Dogs who Eat their Droppings

Almost without exception, when a dog eats his own waste matter, or indeed that of another animal, the owner is appalled and revolted, thinking perhaps that they have a perverted dog on their hands.

The correct term for this practice is coprophagia and it is quite common, not only amongst dogs but many other animals as well. Young puppies often exhibit this behaviour, much to the distress of their owners. A bitch with her litter naturally cleans up after her pups, but this does not mean she is always going to do it, even after her pups have gone to their new homes.

Although this habit is usually just a learned behaviour which is self-rewarding, i.e. the dog sees the droppings simply as extra food, I would advise owners to get their dogs checked out by the vet, just in case there is a physiological cause. There are various conditions which may contribute to the dog developing this habit, such as vitamin or mineral deficiency, pancreatic insufficiency, malnutrition, a low roughage diet, parasitic burden or hyperthyroidism. If the problem is either medical or diet based, then treatment should cure the problem.

Assuming that there is no obvious cause for the behaviour other than habit, there are one or two things you can try. If the dog is only eating his own droppings, then obviously swift removal as they are deposited will prevent him from eating them. Adding a couple of herrings (the tinned variety) to each meal can sometimes work – apparently once herring has been through the digestion process, it becomes extremely unpleasant to the taste when attempts are made to re-ingest it! I have known this to work with some dogs. I have also heard of the same procedure working by using tinned pineapple added to the dog's food.

If the dog is eating the droppings of other dogs, it is very difficult to stop. In my experience, chastising the dog simply makes him quicker or more furtive, but doesn't stop the problem. Putting a muzzle on the dog will physically prevent him, but you will then have the problem of everyone assuming that your dog is aggressive. The good news is that, generally, eating other dogs' droppings will not do the dog any harm, other than making him more susceptible to worm infestation. This is easily counteracted by stepping up the worming treatment to a monthly basis. It is also a good idea to pay closer attention to cleaning the dog's teeth, as the bacteria in the droppings could lead to more dental problems.

Most dogs will also attempt to eat cat droppings, rabbit droppings, horse droppings and the droppings of wild animals such as deer. Remember that this is normal dog behaviour, and try not to get too stressed about it!

Rolling

Rolling in animal droppings, or indeed other foul smelling substances, is another example of how our dogs unwittingly offend us. We think of it as dirty, disgusting behaviour. To a dog though, it is a normal, instinctive part of his canine personality.

One of the most commonly accepted reasons for this behaviour is that, in dog language, the stronger and more pungent he smells, the more superior he appears to another dog. This desire to smell more powerful than other dogs reverts back to when dogs were wild creatures running in packs. The pack leader would wish to impress on his subordinates that he was still top dog. Or perhaps a dog lower in the pecking order would attempt to challenge the pack leader, so to give him added courage, he would first roll in strong smelling animal droppings.

Although our pet dogs have been domesticated for centuries, the desire and instinct to cover themselves in, to us, evil smells is still very strong, even though they may not know why they are doing it. It could occur because you are still having a tussle with your dog as to who is boss, so the dog reverts to his instinctive behaviour in an attempt to impress you.

Our reaction to our smelly dogs is firstly to reject them, not wanting them to get near us and secondly, to bath them as soon as possible to get rid of the smell. This can in turn merely heighten the desire for the dog to repeat his rolling actions as soon as he gets the chance.

As with everything that we wish to deter the dog from doing, you can, through corrective training on the lead, show the dog that you do not like his behaviour. The bad news, though, is that in my experience, a determined 'roller' will generally remain so.

3

FORMAL TRAINING

Formal training is the process of teaching your dog to perform certain actions in response to certain stimuli. It means putting a collar and lead on the dog and conditioning him to respond instantly to your command.

Types of Collars and Leads
The first step is to select the right collar and lead. I would recommend you use a good quality leather lead, at least three feet long, with a strong trigger type clip for attaching the lead to the collar. Rope and nylon leads do not have the same flexible quality as leather and they can 'burn' your hands if pulled through quickly. As to collars, there are many types available:

TRAINING CHAINS. The training chain, or choke chain, is not favoured by most dog trainers and behaviourists. In extreme cases, incorrect fitting and usage can cause damage to the dog's neck. It certainly should NEVER be used on young puppies. Some experienced people do know how to use the chain correctly, but it is not necessary for a pet dog, and other softer collars are now available. However, because they *are* in use, the following information and diagrams are included on selecting a suitable one for your dog, fitting it and how to place it around the dog's neck.

The close-welded link variety is best, as it tends to run more

Fig. 2. Incorrect (left) and correct (right) adjustment for a chain collar.

freely through the links at each end. (The open link variety can jam up.) The correct thickness is important – too thin and you will cut the dog's neck, too thick and it will be too heavy for the dog. When the chain is around the dog's neck, and adjusted so that it fits snugly (but NOT tightly), there should be about a hand's width of chain left, before it attaches to the lead.

To put the chain on, position the dog next to you by your left leg, both of you facing the same direction. Form the collar into a circle by threading it through one metal ring. With the end that is going to be attached to the lead uppermost, slip the chain over the dog's head. Attach the lead to the free ring and, to check that you have it on correctly, use the lead to GENTLY tighten the collar, then relax the pressure. The collar should slacken instantly. If it doesn't, then the collar is on 'upside down'.

Finally, I repeat: the use of chain collars is unnecessary. Better and kinder collars are available.

DOUBLE ACTION TRAINING COLLAR. In my experience, this is the best type of training collar, suitable for the majority of dogs, including puppies. It is made of flat nylon, which is formed into a circle using a connection of a small length of chain, each

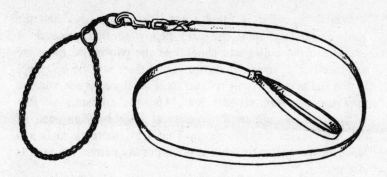

Fig. 3. A chain collar with a suitable leather lead.

end of the chain attaching to the nylon via a metal ring, with a third metal ring in the middle of the chain, for attaching the collar to the lead.

These collars are adjustable and come in various sizes, so they are suitable for the smallest of breeds to the largest. Make sure that you get the type with two adjusters on it – you can buy them with only one adjuster, but these tend to slip and consequently need adjusting frequently.

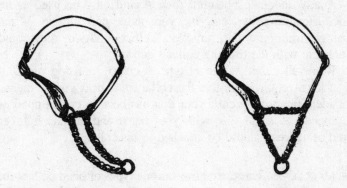

Fig. 4. A double action training collar showing (left) incorrect and right (correct) adjustment.

When the collar is fitted around the dog's neck and the lead is attached, pull the lead gently so that pressure is applied to the collar and check that the two metal rings are not meeting. If they are, it means that there will be no 'give' in the collar and it will remain tight whether or not you are applying pressure via the lead. Use the adjusters so that when you do tighten the collar, at least half an inch of chain separates the two rings. That way, there is sufficient slack in the collar to relax it once pressure from the lead is stopped.

ROPE AND NYLON SLIP COLLARS. These collars are quite satisfactory once you have achieved control over your dog, but are not recommended to begin your training. They tend not to release very quickly; they keep the pressure on the dog's neck even after you have slackened the lead. This could have an adverse effect and actually hinder the training.

ORDINARY LEATHER COLLARS. You should not try to teach my methods of training using an ordinary collar. These collars only put pressure on the front part of the dog's neck and could end up choking him. Once the dog is controlled, they are perfectly adequate but until then should only be used as an identification collar, carrying your name and address. When using a training collar, remove all other collars or they could interfere with the training collar's action.

Remember that, whatever type of collar your dog wears, it is a legal requirement that the collar must bear visible means of identification (even if your dog has been micro-chipped or tattooed). A small disc with your name and contact number and/or address should be attached to his collar.

HEAD COLLARS. There are now various types of head collars for dogs on the market. In some circumstances they can be helpful, but generally speaking you should not need them if you follow the advice given in this book. If you decide that you need one of these head collars, please use it in accordance with the maker's instructions, and, if at all unsure, take advice from a Dog Behaviourist.

BODY HARNESSES. A harness may be recommended for a dog for medical reasons, e.g. if the dog has a neck problem. Unless it is for such a reason, I see no benefit in using one.

How to use the Collar and Lead

The lead and collar are used as a legal requirement and to ensure your dog is with you when you train him! But don't rely on them alone to keep your dog with you. If you simply 'hang on' to him to prevent him either pulling you or wandering off he will just pull even more. As soon as you apply a pulling pressure on the collar, it will make him fight the pressure and try to pull away. Since in some exercises you will be putting a *VERY* gentle *momentary* squeeze on the collar, it is vital that you have the correct type at the start.

Although you must not rely on the lead to control your dog there should never be a time when you take him out of the house or garden without being attached to you, via the lead, however well-trained he eventually becomes. Apart from being an offence to have your dog off a lead on a main road, it is stupid and potentially very dangerous to allow him to walk free on *any* road. There is always a chance that he could be startled into doing something unpredictable, or be frightened into dashing into the road. As well as risking his life, he could endanger the lives of other animals, or worse, other humans.

If, like me, you are a car driver, you may well have experienced the dilemma of seeing a dog walking along off the lead, with the owner several yards away. You have your foot hovering over the brake pedal, wondering if he's about to dash into the road. As the driver of a potentially lethal machine, you may well be put into the position of swerving or braking to avoid the dog, and in the process hit some innocent pedestrian, or at the very least damage someone else's property. Dog owners are now held responsible for any damage their dogs cause, even indirectly, and it could be a very expensive lesson to learn, both for the owner's pocket and his conscience.

Tones of Voice and Visual Signals

As your voice is one of the most important training aids you are going to use, do remember that your dog does not understand the English language. He hears 'sounds' not words, so in theory you can use any word you choose to fit any action, as long as you are consistent. However, it is more realistic for us to use a word that makes sense to us, so we use the word **sit** to get the dog to sit, etc. The tone of the word must be decisive. You don't need to bellow like a sergeant-major, but your voice should convey determination and authority, with you 'telling' your dog, rather than 'asking' him. Each command must also sound different for each separate action.

After each command you will be rewarding your dog, so use lots of excited, loving sounds, such as 'good dog', 'super dog', 'clever dog' etc., all said in a really happy voice. *Show* him with your hands that you are pleased with him, stroke him lovingly, play with him, let him see that his action of compliance has really pleased you. Praise and reward are *vital* to his learning. Reward every effort, however small.

Some exercises will eventually lead to your controlling your dog when he is some distance away from you, so you will be teaching a visual command as well as a verbal one. If you only train with verbal commands you could, for example, have quite a problem getting your dog back to you when he is 200 yards away and the wind is blowing your voice back in the opposite direction. Or suppose you lose your voice – does that mean you also lose control over your dog? Some dogs become deaf as they grow old. Must that mean he can then do as he pleases, because he can no longer hear you?

By giving him audible and visual signals, he has an even better chance of understanding what you want him to do, so that you are not totally dependent on the lead for control.

Getting the Dog to Pay Attention – Watch

By necessity, this has to be the first lesson. Even if you do everything perfectly, all the signalling and commands will be wasted if the dog is not watching you to begin with. You will be incorporating this exercise into all the others you will be teaching, getting him to 'watch' you before giving him any other command.

The aim is to get him to watch you and nothing else, for at least twenty-five seconds at any one time, without moving his head away *at all*. Lack of attention is one of the biggest problems which everyone has when they start training, so it is worth spending time teaching him to watch, before you progress to any of the other exercises. The verbal aids you use are his name, which he should know better than any other sound, and the command **watch me**. You can start teaching him when there are no other distractions and on the occasion when your dog has deliberately chosen to come and seek your attention.

At some time, perhaps when you are sitting watching television, your dog comes over to you, nudges your hand with his nose and 'asks' you for attention. When this happens, gently guide him around so that he is sitting leaning against your left leg. With your right hand under his chin and your left hand on top of his head, stroke and tickle his head, into your left leg and upwards so that you have eye contact. At the same time, tell him **good boy, watch me**. All the time he is gazing up at you, continue to reward him, repeating the command **watch me**, speaking to him in a soothing voice and telling him how good he is.

Having started laying the foundations of this exercise, the next step is to put him on his lead and get him to watch, whilst sitting 'formally' by your left leg. Hold the lead in your right hand, and shorten it by about a quarter – making sure that by doing so you are not putting any pressure on the collar. Have a tit-bit in your left hand, show it to the dog then position the tit-bit at about hip height, in front of your left leg and close to your body, saying the words **watch me**. You will find that the dog's nose will follow the food, causing his head to tip upwards, watching you. Keep him watching you by talking softly to him, then give him the tit-bit *whilst he is still sitting and watching*.

When he has watched for ten seconds, release him from the exercise and allow him to play. By releasing him, I mean making it clear to the dog that he is off duty and work has finished until you command him again. I teach my dogs a release command, namely **that'll do** and they know that when they hear that sound, they can relax and play. Allow him to play, with you participating, for at least two minutes, then get him back under control and repeat the whole process again. You can, if you wish, also teach him a command that means 'back on duty', by saying, 'work' or something similar, but if you teach him from the outset that when you tell him **watch me**, he is on duty, that should be sufficient for him to know that he is about to be commanded to perform some action.

Do the whole exercise three or four times for the first day, with two-minute play breaks between each session. On the second day, repeat as before; this time making him watch for fifteen seconds. Continue over three or four days until he will watch for twenty-five seconds without being distracted.

Sit and Sit Stay
Verbal Command – Dog's name and **sit**.
Visual Signal for **sit** – Right hand raising up in front of dog's nose.
Visual Signal for **stay** – Right hand, palm open towards dog, in front of dog's nose.

Teaching your dog to sit is the most basic of all the training exercises that your dog needs to learn. You have probably already started, with varying degrees of success. You may have found that he will sit when you say, but gets up when *he* wants, not when you say. Or he may sit, but only where *he* wants to. Obviously, if you are starting with a puppy, the following advice will be easier for you, but even if you have an older dog, you can still go back to basics, knowing that once you have made the instruction to sit crystal clear, your dog will always sit when and where you want him to.

Initially, you are not going to say anything to your dog – you are going to see if he can 'work-out' what it is you want him to do, simply by the way you position your right hand. At this stage there is no need to have the dog on a lead. With a tit-bit held between your thumb and first two fingers, palm upwards, hold your hand about an inch out in front of the dog's nose and then raise your hand a few inches (Fig. 5.) Say nothing. The dog will lean forwards to sniff what is in your hand, and as you raise your hand his head will tilt up. If you then move your hand *slightly* back over the dog's head, he will sit. (Fig. 6.) The second his rear end touches the ground, give him the tit-bit, tell him 'clever dog, good sit', and give him a cuddle, telling him 'that'll do'.

Don't worry if he doesn't get the idea immediately, and don't be tempted to hurry things along by 'helping' him to sit, by putting your hand on his rear end and pushing. That will probably only distract him and prolong the whole thing. He

Fig. 5. *Sit* – dog standing, hand holding tit-bit, level with dog's nose.

Fig. 6. *Sit* – dog sitting in front of handler, getting tit-bit.

will get the idea, provided you are patient. I once did this routine with a dog and it took over five minutes with me just holding the tit-bit – and five minutes seems like forever in that situation! The dog must work out for himself just *what* he has to do to get the tit-bit, and it is that 'thinking' process which will cement the exercise in his head. He may well try all sorts of things out – lying down, jumping up, giving a paw, barking, but eventually, the penny will drop!

If he keeps trying to jump up to get the tit-bit, it's probably because you are holding it a little too high above his nose, either initially or as he tries to take it. Lower your hand slightly and keep it still, and that will sort out the problem.

So, persevere. Once he's got the hang of it, repeat exactly the same routine three times. On the fourth time, as you raise your hand up, tell him **sit**. Now you are turning the situation around, getting him to sit when *you* say. As long as you give the tit-bit and praise immediately he sits, the learning process will accelerate quickly.

You may find that he wants to get up as soon as you have

given the tit-bit. Provided you are sure that he now understands what **sit** means, keep him sitting for a few seconds
before you give the tit-bit and praise. Don't be tempted to say
stay just yet. You want him to be rock solid sitting beside or in
front of you, before you progress to the next step.

Once you have him sitting every time, off the lead, now go
to the next stage, sitting beside your left leg, on the lead.
Guide him gently beside your leg, using the tit-bit, held as
previously described, to encourage him to the correct position.
Hold the lead in whichever hand feels more comfortable to
you, tit-bit in right hand, and make sure that you are not
putting any pressure, via the lead, onto the collar. Now he is
beside you, you will need to position your right arm across
your body, so that your hand is held just in front of, and
slightly above the dog's head. Try to imagine the position your
right arm would be in if it were in a sling, and you'll have it in
the right place! (Fig. 7.)

Now take one step forward, with the dog, stop and tell him

Fig. 7. *Sit* – dog sitting on handler's left, handler's right arm across body,
giving dog tit-bit.

to **sit**, raising your right hand slightly as you stop. He will sit! Give him the tit-bit, praise, making sure he doesn't get up, keep him there for a couple of seconds, then break off and play. Repeat this several times, until you can go forward one step, stop, sit, praise, continue for another step, etc., for at least five steps.

You may find that as you stop each time, the dog will sit but slightly creeps around to get in front of you, swinging his rear end out. If this is the case, rather than walking in a straight line, make each step into a very gentle left-handed curve, so that you are *slightly* turning into your dog on each step. Another way of stopping this type of problem is to walk beside a straight wall, with the dog between you and the wall, starting with the dog literally touching the wall. This will physically prevent the dog from swinging around.

If he is coming too far forward, it is probably because you are holding the tit-bit out a bit too far. Bringing your arm in closer to your body should stop this happening.

You have now taught your dog to sit each and every time you say so, whether he is on or off lead, and whether he is in front of you (off lead) or beside you (on or off lead). As an additional bonus, you have also made a gentle start on teaching heelwork (see page 77), plus you have started to condition him that each time you stop, he is to sit. Now you can teach him to sit and *stay*.

SIT-STAY. Why should he learn to stay? Of course, if you want to enter obedience competitions, this is one of the exercises he will have to do. Even if you have no aspirations ever to take your dog into the ring, it is a good exercise to teach, both from the point of view of giving you more overall control, and also because it has some practical applications. The most obvious to me is when a visitor calls, and the front door is opened. I like my dog to accompany me to the door, especially at night, but I don't want him running through it, either to greet the visitor, or going past the visitor out onto the road. Teaching him to sit and stay a couple of feet back from the door whilst I go forward and open it is therefore important.

So, to teach this exercise formally, have your dog on his lead, sitting by your left leg, holding the lead loosely in your left hand. Whenever you are leaving your dog in either a sit or a down, always move right foot first. Although your dog will not realise at this early stage, you are going to be conditioning the dog that whenever the right foot moves first, he is to remain behind. When the left foot moves first, he is to come with you. It is an added signal to the dog, to prepare him for what is about to happen.

Tell the dog to **stay** in a gentle but firm voice, and start to move your *right* foot forward, as though you were going to step away, but *don't*. (Fig. 8.) Just keep moving your right foot backwards and forwards, repeating the stay command as necessary, for about ten seconds. Assuming he has made no attempt to move, tell him 'good sit stay, clever dog', in a calm and loving tone. Provided he has not moved, next take a proper step forward, stepping straight round and facing your dog, right up close to his front feet. Remain there for about

Fig. 8. *Sit, Stay* – dog sitting on left, handler moving right foot.

five seconds, repeat the stay command and return back to the side of your dog, and stand still. Wait another couple of seconds, all the time telling him calmly 'good dog', etc., then give him a gentle stroke on the top of his head, again with verbal praise. He must still be sitting and staying right up to this point.

You are then going to release him, as you have already taught him in the 'watch' exercise, but this time with a difference. You will take a step *backwards* and encourage your dog to turn into you, thereby also moving *backwards*. If he is conditioned that the only way to move after the command of sit, stay, is to go backwards, he is far less likely to 'break' the stay by coming forwards. So move backwards, taking him with you, saying 'that'll do, clever boy', etc., stroking and cuddling him.

Repeat this stage of the exercise several times, gradually increasing the time you are standing in front, until he is perfectly relaxed with you leaving his side and standing in front of him for at least 10-15 seconds. Up to this point, you will have been holding the lead at all times, but now, start detaching the lead before you leave him. Don't leave the lead connected to his collar and simply drop it on the floor. This will actually encourage him to lie down, as he will be tempted to sniff or investigate the lead hanging in front of him, and may 'follow' his nose down to the floor. So practise without the lead first, until you can again stand in front for 10-15 seconds, then you can begin to increase both the distance and length of time you can leave your dog. (Fig. 9.)

If you do the whole exercise over seven days, by day seven, you should be able to get 4-6 feet in front, for about a minute. Build it up day by day and step by step, don't be tempted to rush any part. Unless you are training to compete in obedience competition, you don't need to try for any more distance or time – what you have taught is quite adequate for the pet dog.

When you have reached the position of him sitting and staying for the required time and distance, start to leave him at different angles, i.e. step behind him instead of in front, or step

Fig. 9.   *Sit, Stay* – hand signal from the front.

out sideways. Walk around your dog whilst he is sitting. All these things will add to the stability of the exercise.

DO'S AND DON'TS. When teaching the exercise on the lead, make sure that when you step in front of your dog you don't put any tension or movement on the lead. Obviously, if you do, the dog is likely to get up, as he will interpret the lead movement as a signal for *him* to move.

Don't use the dog's name when you are standing in front of him – again, he associates his name with movement, and may get up. You *can* talk to him to reassure him that he is doing it right, but just avoid using his name.

Don't stare into your dog's eyes when you are standing in front of him. A direct stare could also encourage him to get up – look at a point between his ears, that way you can still watch him without having eye contact.

If the dog moves, don't punish him! Gently 'chide' him, i.e. 'silly dog', etc., and start again. If you punish him for moving, it will make him uneasy about the whole exercise, and you want him to feel happy about staying, rather than tense.

Do make it clear that by staying, he is pleasing you. Tell him softly what a clever dog he is – not in a loud, excited voice, which may encourage him to move, but rather in a gentle, loving voice.

Down

Verbal Command – Dog's name and **down**.

Visual Signal – Right hand level with dog's head, then lower hand to the floor.

To lie down for you is an act of submission on the part of the dog, so you should try to make it as pleasant as possible, bearing in mind that the dog could see it as 'losing face'. You may have noticed that when two strange dogs confront one another, one dog will sometimes lie down, often rolling right over on his back. This is a submissive act, showing the standing dog that the lying down dog recognises him as being dominant, and that the submissive dog poses no threat to him. Each time your dog lies down for you, your dog is sending you a similar message.

Before you even begin teaching him on the lead to lie down, you can start to condition him to the sound of the command, i.e. **down**, by cheating a little. Every time you see your dog about to lie down naturally, as he starts to 'bend', give him the down command, and praise him. Once he's down, repeat the verbal command again, saying 'what a good **down**, clever dog, good **down**', etc. He will quickly associate his, albeit voluntary, act of lying down with praise and reward from you, together with the sound of the command **down**.

You then progress to showing the dog where and when you want him to lie down. Put him on his lead, and with him sitting beside your left leg, hold the lead in your left hand. Have a tit-bit in your right hand. Go down on one knee beside the dog.

Hold the tit-bit between your thumb and first two fingers, and 'show' the dog the tit-bit, an inch or so in front of and level with his nose. Then take the tit-bit, still in your fingers, straight down to the floor and keep it still. (Fig. 10.) Make sure that your hand is palm downwards, with the tit-bit covered by your fingers. *Do not say anything*. The dog's head will naturally follow the tit-bit to the floor. Once his nose is level with your hand on the floor, carefully slide your hand about two inches straight out level with his nose. *Do not say anything*. After a few seconds the dog will 'drop' his front legs and lie down. As he does so, and *whilst he is still lying down*, give him the tit-bit and tell him 'good **down**, clever dog', etc. (Fig. 11.) Keep him there for a few seconds by continuing to praise him and if necessary give him another tit-bit, then tell him **'that'll do'**, stand up and encourage him to get up too.

After repeating the above a few more times, only saying the down command once he is lying down, you can now start using the **down** sound as you lower the tit-bit to the floor.

Fig. 10. *Down* – dog sitting by left leg, with handler kneeling by dog, hand holding tit-bit going to floor.

Fig. 11. *Down* – dog lying down, handler giving tit-bit.

Very quickly he will start to follow your hand and your voice command. Say the command nicely but with a gentle authority – don't bellow, and don't make it sound like a punishment.

POSSIBLE PROBLEMS. One of the commonest problems when you start teaching the down command is that as the dog's head follows the tit-bit to the floor, its back end comes up. Don't continue trying to get the dog to lie down from the standing position. Give him the sit command, and start again. Eventually, once the command has been learnt, he will happily lie down from standing up, but to begin with it is a hard concept for him to take in.

HAVING AN UNPLEASANT ASSOCIATION WITH BEING TOLD TO LIE DOWN. Perhaps in the past the dog has been told to lie down in a punishing tone, or even been physically forced to lie down, either by being pushed, or worse still, having his front legs pulled out to make him drop to the ground. He will by now have built up an unpleasant association with being told to lie down. If that is the case, I would suggest that you choose another sound command – perhaps the word **flat** or **floor**. Changing the command sound will take away the initial unpleasant connection and may help to stop the dog from 'stiffening up' when he hears the command. You will need to be on a non-carpeted surface, either lino or floorboards. Kneel down beside the dog, and cuddle him into your left side. Be prepared to be very patient, if necessary cuddling him up to you for several minutes. When he relaxes, you will find he will be leaning into your body. With the tit-bit positioned as before, slowly and gently slide your left leg back, and as you do so the dog will slide gently and gracefully to the floor. Give him praise and the tit-bit immediately, cuddle him, tickle his tummy, etc. Keep repeating the command you have chosen, saying 'good **floor**, clever dog, what a good **floor**'. Anyone who doesn't realise what is happening will of course think you are truly mad, telling the floor how good it is, but *you* know what you are doing, and remember, it's not the word the dog is learning, it's the *sound*.

SETTLE. Having taught your dog to lie down beside you, it is a fairly easy step to command your dog to go and **settle** down, away from you. I'm sure you can think of an occasion when you are sitting, perhaps watching television and, after giving your dog a cuddle, you want him to go away and lie down, rather than lie at your feet. Or, after a visitor has arrived, and you want to entertain your guest, you don't want the dog under your feet.

When you decide that it's time for him to go and settle, stop touching him and say, gently but firmly 'that's enough, go **settle** down'. If you reduce all contact, you will find that after a few seconds the dog will walk away from you, choosing where to settle, and lie down. As he does so, say softly 'good dog'. If you say the praise too excitedly, it will encourage him to come back to your side for more attention. If you repeat that over a period of a few days, you will eventually be able just to say '**go settle**', and he will 'put himself away' quite happily.

Down, Stay

Verbal Command – Dog's name and down, **stay**.

Visual Signal – Left hand, palm open facing dog, in front of dog's nose.

Once your dog has learnt to lie down when you say so, the next stage is for him to remain down, whilst you stand up, and eventually walk away. Don't attempt to teach the stay until you know your dog understands the down and is comfortable in that position, rather than attempting to 'spring' back up. The need to teach him to lie down and stay down are the same as previously mentioned in the sit and stay, plus it gives the dog another 'string to his bow'.

Having told him to lie down, with you kneeling by his side, and holding the lead in your right hand, deliver the verbal and visual signals calmly, and start to stand up. Take care not to put any pressure on the collar, via the lead, as you stand up. (Fig. 12.) Any movement of the lead could result in your dog

Fig. 12. *Down, Stay* – the visual signal.

misinterpreting that movement as a signal for him to get up. If he should attempt to follow you, repeat the down, stay command, in a gentle but firm voice. Once you are standing, remain there for five seconds, then kneel back down to your dog, saying 'good down **stay**', etc., in a loving tone, then after a couple of seconds, release and reward.

Repeat this several times, until he is perfectly relaxed about you getting up whilst he stays down. Then progress to the next stage, which you do in exactly the same way as you taught the sit, stay, moving your right foot first, as if to take a step, etc. The obvious difference is that you say **down**, stay.

The routine differs from the sit, stay, when you return to the side of your dog. Having waited a couple of seconds at the side, *go down to his level* to give him a gentle reward, and then release him from the stay by saying 'that'll do', and allowing him to get up.

If he only gets the reward in the down position, he will not anticipate the reward by jumping up.

Follow the same teaching pattern as you did for the sit, stay, over a period of seven days, making your ultimate aim a one minute down, stay, 4-6 feet away.

Again, as with the sit, stay, when you reach the position of him staying down whilst you stand a few feet in front of him, start leaving him at different angles, i.e. step behind him, rather than in front, or step out sideways. Start walking around your dog whilst he is staying down. All these things will add to the stability of the stay exercise.

A final DON'T. Please never use the down, stay as a form of punishment, e.g. 'go to your basket and stay down'. You want him to enjoy staying down, but if he relates it to being in your bad books, he will start to break the stay, as he will feel uneasy and unhappy in that position, associating it with being in the wrong.

THE 'QUICK' DOWN AND STAY. Having taught your dog to lie down and stay, it can be very useful if you can get your dog to 'drop' instantly and stay. From a control point of view, if the dog ever gets over excited, perhaps during a play session, it can be a very effective stop switch. In an emergency situation, a dog that will drop and stay instantly is much safer than one who is careering about, perhaps in the traffic.

You can teach the quick down as a game, either using a toy or a bumper tit-bit. If your dog likes playing with toys, select his favourite one, and keep it just for this exercise. If toys don't hold much interest for him, have some special tit-bits in your hand. Have your dog on his lead, and start getting him excited with the toy (or tit-bit), just keeping it out of his reach and gently 'goading' him with it. Say 'what's this' and 'what have I got, do you want it?', all the time twisting and turning round in a tight circle, just keeping it away from him. After about 10-15 seconds, take your hand with the toy or tit-bit, straight down to the floor, as in the visual down signal, and give the verbal down command. Your dog will probably 'pounce' downwards onto the reward. Refrain from giving it to him for a couple of seconds, repeating over and over 'good down, clever dog, good down', etc., then let him have the reward. Very quickly he will learn that by 'throwing' himself down, he gets the treat or the toy. If using a toy, let him play with it for a few seconds; if using tit-bits, give him another couple, then repeat the whole exercise.

To further reinforce this exercise, make him do a quick down before you put his lead on when taking him for a walk. If he builds up a pleasant association with the quick down, i.e. food, toy or going out, he will always want to comply.

Coming When Called – The Recall
Verbal Command – Dog's name followed by **come**.
Visual Signal – Arms outstretched, either side of your body.

You should have already built the groundwork for this exercise by calling your dog each time you feed him, as suggested in Chapter 2. You will have started to condition the dog to return to you when he hears the sound **come**, by being rewarded for obeying – albeit so far because he wants his dinner!

If you haven't yet established that groundwork, you cannot expect your dog to come when called *outside* if he doesn't come instantly when called *inside*. Sometimes you may have allowed him to ignore your call in the house, or you may have called him two or three times before he has responded. Up to now it has not seemed important, as he can't get into any danger or annoy anyone else by not returning to you immediately. Unfortunately, if you have allowed the dog to return to you indoors in his own time, he will simply transfer that behaviour to outside, when he is off the lead and enjoying himself. Bearing in mind that he may be playing with another dog, or having a good sniff, or eating something revolting, all of which to the dog are much more exciting and/or interesting than returning to you, it is therefore hardly surprising that you have to call him several times before he returns – after all, you have permitted such behaviour indoors.

So, how do you turn that situation around. Firstly, you must ensure the instant response indoors. Always use food as a reward – in fact make the dog earn ALL his daily food

Fig. 13. *Come* – the hand signal.

ration by coming when called. Make up his daily allowance into at least 20 portions, so you can call him at least 20 times during the day for a food based reward. Start using the visual signal previously described, and initially call him to you when he is very close by, so that he can *see* the reward that is waiting for him. If he doesn't respond *immediately*, discard that portion of food – he doesn't get what he doesn't earn. At the end of the first day he may have earned half of his food, possibly more, but the following day he will be a bit hungrier, so will probably earn more. Continue with this until he is earning all his daily food allowance by coming immediately you call him.

In some instances, where the dog has learned to ignore you indoors, it may be a good idea to incorporate a new attention sound along with the above. If he is ignoring his own name when used as part of the recall, try using an ordinary whistle (not a special dog whistle), just before you call him to 'Come'. If he learns to associate the sound of the whistle with food, he will come to the whistle outside too. (This type of conditioning was researched by an eminent

Fig. 14. The dog responds.

scientist called Pavlov, who discovered that by turning a light on each time he fed his dogs, he noticed that he could get the dogs to salivate *just* by switching on the light, without any food being offered – the dogs associating the light with the *prospect* of being fed.)

Once you have tuned the dog into the whistle, try adding his name after you have blown the whistle. Eventually you may well be able to dispense with the whistle, as you will have re-conditioned the same response to his name, as to the whistle.

Each and every time the dog responds, either indoors or outside, to the signal to return to you, he must get his reward, both edible and physical. Even if he has only returned from a couple of yards away, show him how pleased you are by cuddling and praising him. Always put a hand on his collar first – this is for two reasons. One, it shows that you have control and two, if you don't, he may well snatch the food and run off again.

It also gives you an opportunity to show the dog that by returning to you, he gets confined for a few seconds, but then *you let him go again.* If you only ever call him to you when it's time for the walk/fun/playtime to end, he will very quickly decide he doesn't want to come back. If you call him to you many times during the walk, each time holding his collar and then letting him go, he will never get into the habit of knowing when the walk is over. Give him a signal when you let him go each time – something like 'go play' or 'off you go'.

When the walk is over, don't always call him at the same spot in the park. He will quickly learn the route of his walk, and will start to associate 'that spot' with the end of his freedom, and may well start to run off or ignore you when you get to the usual place.

POSSIBLE PROBLEMS. If your dog has previously learned that when he is off the lead he can ignore you, even if he comes every time you call him indoors, don't fall into the trap of chasing him, or trying to grab him. He will be much quicker than you can be, and, from the dog's perception, it becomes a game which he always wins. *NEVER* tell him off once he does deign to return to you. From your viewpoint, you are telling the dog off for not returning immediately, and making you wait, possibly being late for work, or an appointment (they always seem to know when you're in a hurry, don't they!). From the dog's perception, he has finally decided to give up playing with another dog, or chasing rabbits, or digging a hole, etc., and when he gets back to you, you're cross! Rather than being pleased to see him, you tell him off, maybe, heaven forbid, you smack him! What does he learn? Returning to you is UNPLEASANT. Staying away from you is far more rewarding.

There are some things you can do in that situation. STOP calling him – he's ignoring you anyway. If safe to do so, walk away from the dog. (Obviously if he's close to a road, that is not a good idea.) Sit on the grass and pretend to be ever so interested in something on the ground right in front of you. Dogs are curious creatures, and he may well come back to see what you are finding so fascinating. When he does return. DON'T GRAB HIM. Greet him warmly, and offer him a tit-bit, at the same time gently placing your hand on his collar. Reward him profusely, give him another tit-bit and then *let him go again*. If you don't, he definitely won't come back the next time you let him off his lead.

If a dog has had an unpleasant experience in the past connected with coming when called, or because of poor training has learnt not to come back, you may need to resort to putting him on a long line – about fifty feet – and letting him trail that behind him, so that you can either take hold, or stand on it, to prevent the dog from running off. It is not ideal though, and often once you let them off the line, they immediately return to their old habits. You may ultimately have to opt for a compromise, and keep your dog on an extending lead – that way at least the dog can run a short way and have some freedom of movement. The down exercise, on page 60 can help in some cases when dogs won't come back, so read it carefully.

Wait
Verbal Command – Dog's name and **wait**.
Visual Signal – One sweep of the left arm, starting from the side of your left leg, over in front of the dog's face – like the pendulum swing of a clock.

Having taught your dog that **stay** means 'stay where I tell you until I come back to you', you now need to teach him that **wait** means, 'wait where I tell you until I give you further commands'. For example, **wait** whilst the door is opened before he jumps out of the car; **wait** whilst the front door is opened properly, rather than trying to push through it half

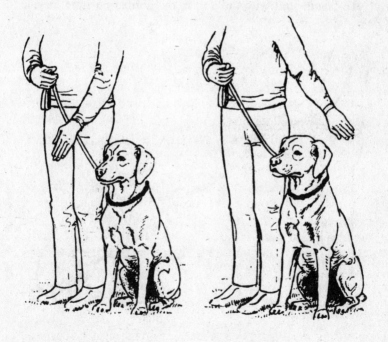

Fig. 15. *Wait* – the hand signal.

opened; **wait** while you put his dinner on the floor, etc.

Some people teach the **stay** to cover all these things, plus staying in one place, but I firmly believe this confuses the dog, giving him one command to mean two different things and expecting him to know which one you mean. It also encourages him to break the **stay** exercise, as he will be continually on edge, waiting for further commands. If you have taught him that **stay** means he *never* moves until you return to his side, there can be no doubt in his mind whatsoever. With the **wait**, you are teaching him that he is to wait until given further instruction.

A word of caution before you start. Please don't practise the **stay** and **wait** exercises one after the other. You don't want to give your dog any chance of becoming confused. Even though the command is different, at the beginning there is a risk that he may try and anticipate your wishes.

To begin, start with the dog in the normal position, beside

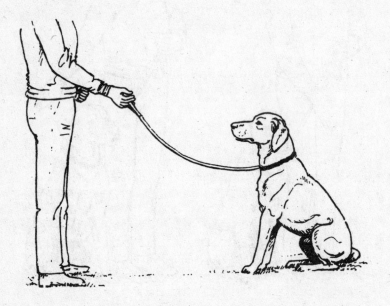

Fig. 16. Dog waiting.

your left leg. Remember to leave him right foot first, give him the verbal and visual **wait** commands and step to the front of him. Remain there for a couple of seconds, then repeat the verbal command and back away from him, until you are at the end of the lead (fig. 16). Stand still and call him to you, rewarding him as he comes.

If he should move before you call, correct him very gently by putting him back on the exact spot again. Don't be too harsh with the correction, as, if you over correct, it may put him off moving and make him hesitant when you call him next time. All the time he remains sitting and waiting, tell him gently what a good dog he is – don't get too excited at this stage, otherwise again it may encourage him to move before you want him to.

By telling him gently that he is good for waiting, he will understand quicker what he is supposed to be doing. Repeat this two or three times over a couple of days and then start incorporating the **wait** command whenever the situation is appropriate. Getting out of the car is usually where this exercise is most beneficial – there are few things worse, or potentially more dangerous, than a dog which leaps out of the car the instant the door is open. By teaching him the **wait** exercise properly, you will be able to open the car door and know he will not move until you tell him so.

Stand
Verbal Command – Dog's name and **stand**.

I'm sure that some readers are wondering why on earth they should teach their dog to stand on command and what practical purpose it would serve. Well, how about when you brush your dog? What about when he comes back from a muddy walk and you have to dry him? Think about when you have to take the dog to the vet – it's much easier for the vet to examine him if he's standing nice and still. I'm sure you can think of other occasions within your own lives when it would be very convenient if he stood still on command.

The **stand** is the gentlest of all exercises to teach and also one of the easiest. The verbal command **stand** is given very gently, unlike all other commands you have been using and is delivered in a 'sing-song' type of voice. It must sound completely different from the authoritative commands of **sit** and **down**. The aim is to teach him that on receiving the verbal and visual commands, he will stand up, keeping his front feet still and moving his back feet *backwards*.

Start with your dog sitting on your left, close to your leg. He doesn't need to be on a lead. Have a tit-bit in your right hand, holding it between your thumb and first two fingers. Position your hand so that it is *almost* touching the dog's nose, and then slowly move your hand straight out a couple of inches in front of his nose. (Fig. 17.)

He will want to follow the food, and will stretch out, probably attempting to stand as he does so. Don't say **stand** at this stage, as you again want him to work out what movement is required, as you did when teaching the sit and down. If he doesn't quite get up, place your left hand, between you and him, and gently tickle and lift under his tummy, in an upwards and *slightly* backwards direction. (Fig. 18.)

Fig. 17. *Stand* – dog sitting on left, hand holding tit-bit being extended outward.

Fig. 18. *Stand* – dog starting to follow hand, being gently helped by tummy lift.

As soon as he is standing, give him the food, telling him 'good **stand**, clever dog' several times, and keep him standing still by continuing to tickle his tummy with your left hand, whilst your right hand gently tickles the front of his chest. (Fig. 19.)

He will probably be more than willing to stand there for ever, as he is receiving such lovely inducement to do so! Eventually, you will want him to stand just on the verbal command, perhaps with the hand signal also, which you are teaching with the help of the tit-bit, but practise several times using all the inducements, until he really latches on to the idea. Make sure you keep your voice command light and very pleasant sounding. If you make it too commanding, or gruff, he will get confused and perhaps interpret it the wrong way, perhaps either lying down, or maybe not moving at all, as he is unclear just *what* is expected of him.

You may feel that it would be easier and more comfortable for you if you place your left arm *over* the dog to lift and tickle

Fig. 19. *Stand* – dog standing on left, right hand tickling chest.

him into the position. What tends to happen if you do that is that the dog will lean against the arm that is doing the tickling, resulting in him leaning away from you, and you having to shuffle sideways towards your dog, to keep him with you.

You may find that once he has stood up, he continues to move forwards. That is because you have continued to move your right hand, with the tit-bit, away from his nose. As soon as he has stood, keep your hand still, and he will have no reason to walk away from it – he wants the tit-bit which your hand is holding. Make sure that you don't move your hand either up or down, but keep it straight out in front of the dog when you are encouraging him to stand. Any movement in either direction could again lead to the dog being confused and interpreting the movement as either a sit or a down signal, as he has already learned those hand movements when you taught him those positions.

Finally, you may find it easier if you kneel down beside your dog to begin with when teaching this exercise – it is certainly easier if you have a small dog, but with a dog of any size, it will save you bending over, and being nearer to your dog will make delivery of the hand signal, plus the lifting and tickling, much more definite.

Walking to Heel

Verbal Command – Dog's name (for attention) and initially **steady**. When **steady** has been taught, choose either **heel** or **close**.

Pulling on the lead is second only to recall problems as the exercise that owners seem to have the most trouble with, and I suspect that some of you may have turned straight to these pages, without reading the preceding ones! If you *have* done that, please read the previous pages first, as everything written so far has been designed to help with overall control, culminating in making this exercise easier to teach.

Two of the many reasons why a dog pulls is that being on the lead is boring and restricting. Boring because he cannot keep stopping to investigate and sniff, and restricting because you are trying to make him walk where *you* want, i.e. at your side, rather than where *he* wants to be, i.e. out in front. It tends to become one long battle, with you pulling each other, and each attempt by you to pull him back makes him more determined to pull forward. Sometimes it becomes such an ordeal for owners that they stop trying, either by not putting the dog on the lead at all (extremely foolish and dangerous, not to say against the law if on a road), or by tolerating the dog pulling and keeping the lead walks to a minimum, and ending up with a sore shoulder and arm in the process. Have I struck a chord yet?

So, how can you make walking on the lead a happier process for you both and at the same time teach the dog not to pull? You can't expect the dog to walk forward without pulling if he cannot stand still on the lead without pulling, so that is your starting point. However, before you begin, a word of caution. The twitch type action that I mention later is designed simply to off-balance the dog. *It is not meant to choke him or cause him pain*. It will have the effect of momentarily stopping him. Please don't be heavy handed by jerking, pulling or tugging the lead. Finally, only twitch the lead if you have an adult dog. DO NOT PUT ANY PRESSURE ON A PUPPY'S NECK, just use the verbal command, followed by the praise and the tit-bit.

Have him on the lead, and stand still. Hold the lead in your right hand, making sure that the dog has all the lead length to use. MAKE SURE THAT *YOU* ARE NOT TIGHTENING THE LEAD and do not put both hands on the lead together. You will need your left hand free for praising and giving the tit-bit. As he starts to put tension onto the lead by straining forward, take one small step backwards and give a *VERY GENTLE*, but *VERY QUICK* 'twitch' type action on the lead. As you do so, say **steady**, and the second the pressure comes off the lead and the dog looks at you, give him the **watch** command that you have previously taught him (see page 51), verbally reward profusely and give him a tit-bit instantly. Don't rush with the next step, make sure he realises that you are really pleased with him for not putting tension on the lead. Then repeat with another step forward.

Depending on the determination of the dog, the length of time that he has previously been allowed to pull for, and, importantly, whether he sees you as pack leader or not, will depend on how many individual single steps you have to make. It may be as few as five, it may be as many as one hundred. Until he will happily stand on a loose lead, don't try and take the training any further. At this stage, you are not trying to get him to walk by your leg, you are simply teaching him to walk on a loose lead *without* pulling.

Provided he is now standing happily on a loose lead, now take another step and assuming he doesn't take up the slack on the lead, again reward, verbally and edibly. Now take two steps, then reward. Build up the walking gradually until you can take about six normal paces without having to stop, and without the dog making any attempt to pull. Make sure that *all* the time the dog is walking nicely you are verbally rewarding him, 'good dog, good **steady**, clever dog', etc. And giving him a tit-bit or two. (Fig. 20.)

Fig. 20. *Heel* – dog walking on loose lead, not pulling.

Having achieved six steps without pulling, now you want to show him that sometimes he has to walk closer to you, rather than at the end of the lead. For this, you will need lots of inducement in the shape of tit-bits or, if your dog likes to play with toys, his favourite toy. Decide which command you are going to use, either **heel** (pronounced HEYALL) or **close** (pronounced CLOWSS). Position him sitting on your left, with his right shoulder close to and almost touching your left leg (Fig. 21.) That is the ideal heel position, which you want him to keep to when he is walking. Hold the lead in your right hand, with the tit-bit or toy in your left hand. Place the 'inducement' an inch or so in front of his nose, and step off on your *left* foot, using the command **heel** or **close**. You step off left foot first as an added signal that he is to be with you – remember when teaching the sit and down stay, you always moved right foot first, as he had to remain behind.

After taking two paces, give him the inducement, take a step back and PLAY with him, either interacting with him and the toy, or, if you're not using a toy, have a play just with him.

Fig. 21. *Heel* – prior to starting heel work.

After half a minute or so, set him up again and repeat the two paces. When he is nice and steady doing two paces, do four, then six and so on, building up slowly, over several sessions, until he will walk for twenty or thirty paces beside your left leg, keeping his shoulder level with your leg and not pulling. (Fig. 22.)

All the time he is walking nicely, verbally reward him, tickle him gently on the top of his head, or on his right ear. (Fig. 23.) Tell him how wonderful he is, and, without stopping walking, give him a tit-bit every three or four paces. Tell him, whilst you are walking, what a good heel (or close) he is doing. Remember that you want him to associate the verbal command with his action of walking nicely, so keep repeating it. If you're using a toy, let him have the toy to hold a couple of times during the session, again without stopping walking.

Fig. 22. *Heel* – dog walking by handler's left leg.

Keep the sessions short – no more than ten minutes at the most, two or three times a day. Over about a week, you will have conditioned him to walk properly for all normal requirements. You will have taught him that being on the lead is FUN, as he gets food, and/or a toy. He will be receiving constant, positive attention from you when he remains close to you. There will not be any discomfort for him to fight, as previously when you have had a 'tug of war' with him.

The other positive outcome of teaching him this way is that you will have developed two different modes of walking. One, with the *heel* or *close* command, means that he has to stay next to your left leg, as needed on a busy road, or when there are crowds of people about, and two, with the *steady* command, meaning that as long as he doesn't pull, he can be out at the

Fig. 23. *Heel* – dog walking nicely, getting rewarded.

end of the lead, in circumstances where he would not be causing a nuisance to anyone or be in danger.

POSSIBLE PROBLEMS. If the dog is still trying to pull, it may be that you are causing him to do so, by 'hanging' on to the lead too tightly (see Fig. 24.) You must give him a chance to walk nicely by starting with a loose lead, and immediately you have given him the steady signal, ensure that the lead is loose again. As he attempts to take up the slack of the lead, signal the collar and take a small step to your right simultaneously. This will have the effect of increasing the off-balancing action of the signal.

Perhaps you are holding the lead with your left hand as well as your right (Fig. 25), trying to stop the dog getting in front of you to start with. This is counter-productive, not only because it ties up your left hand, which you need to be free to give the praise and tit-bits, but also because it tends to make you pull

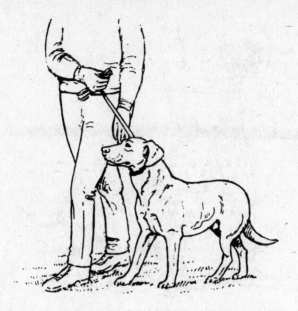

Fig. 24. *Heel* – lead too short.

the lead back with your left hand. Also, even if you are still attempting to give the twitch signal with your right hand, the first object that signal will connect with is your left hand, not the dog!

You may be trying to walk too quickly, so that the dog is trying to race you. The quicker your dog wants to walk, the *slower* you should walk. He is being taught to walk at your pace, not the other way around!

LAGGING. Maybe your dog is nervous when on the lead, perhaps lagging behind you. If that is the case, *do not put any pressure on the collar*. Turn to face him whilst still walking, continue to walk backwards in the same direction, slow your pace and use *loads* of encouragement, clap your hands, offer tit-bits and cuddles and use a reassuring, confident voice. If you try to

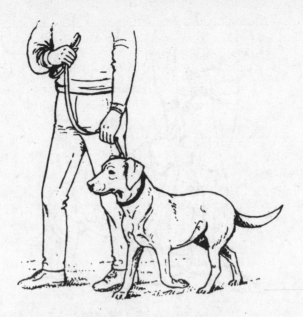

Fig. 25. *Heel* – lead held incorrectly, left hand holding half way up.

'baby' him, he will simply become even more nervous. Adopt the attitude of 'everything's fine, I'm in charge, so nothing nasty is going to happen'. A sort of jolly hockey sticks approach! To make walking on the lead even nicer for him, always put him on the lead before every nice event in his life, i.e. every meal time, and when people he knows come to call. Make the lead the prelude to nice things happening.

GETTING THE DOG TO RETURN TO HEEL FROM ANY POSITION. There will be times when your dog manages to position himself in the wrong place, just as you want to start walking with him. You have probably been 'scooping' him back to your left side with your hands, which will only have made him want to sit incorrectly even more. He likes being touched and so repeats the action which makes you touch him!

Using the commands which, by now, will be meaning **heel** to the dog, you are going to show him how to get there on his own, without your having to touch him. Obviously you will use exactly the same signals as you have been using to teach him to be by your left leg, as this is where you want him to be.

To show him how to move into the correct position, he must first of all be in the wrong one. For the purpose of teaching, start with him sitting in front of you – something which happens very easily if you are too slow with the **sit** command when you come to a halt.

To set this up, incorporate the **wait** command which you have already taught him. Start with him sitting by your left leg, command him to **wait** and step around to face him, close

Fig. 26.   Ready to return to the *heel* position from the front.

to his front feet, as in fig. 26. Now you are going to stand still and he is going to move around behind you, going past your right leg and ending up on your left-hand side.

Gather the slack of the lead up in your right hand, without putting any pressure on the collar, and give him the command which you have already taught him to mean 'be by my left leg'. Have a tit-bit hidden in your *right* hand. At this stage he will probably look confused, as he won't be able to work out *how* to get to your left leg, even though he knows that is where you want him. Pat your left leg with your left hand, and guide the dog towards your right leg, showing him the tit-bit. As soon as his head is level with your right leg, reach around behind you with your left hand and take hold of the lead and the tit-bit, at the same time looking over your left shoulder as far as you can, until you can catch your dog's eye. (See Fig. 27.)

Continue to encourage him round, with your voice and the tit-bit, and as his head appears beside your left leg, change the lead and tit-bit back into your right hand, and as his shoulder

Fig. 27.   Dog being guided around handler, following hand holding tit-bit.

gets level with your left leg, tell him to sit and give him the tit-bit and lots of praise. (See Fig. 28.)

Now, all that is a great deal more complicated to write down than actually do! Follow the pictures carefully and you will see it is quite simple really. It helps if your dog can see your face as he is coming around behind you. Once he is up and moving, turn your head around to your left, so that you can see him coming and greet him as he comes around. Remember to keep your feet still. You must remain stationary; he is moving to you, not you to him.

If you are having trouble getting the initial movement from your dog (i.e. getting him up from the sit position), you can, just to start with, take a step back with your right foot as you give him the first heel signal. This gives you a little more 'impetus'. As soon as he is up and moving, you must put your right foot level with the left one. Don't leave it out behind you, or your dog will have to walk out and around you to get to the heel position, making him go very wide and giving you more trouble in controlling him.

Fig. 28. Dog completing the exercise, being given tit-bit.

When you've practised this exercise a few times and your dog understands what you want, start getting him to come to heel from any direction. Again using the **wait** command, start with him sitting by your left leg, tell him **wait** and step forward one pace, stand still and call him up to heel, using full commands and signals. Again, with him sitting by your left leg, take a step sideways, away from him, then call him to heel, this time continuing to walk forwards as he comes to you.

If you are determined and patient, and don't try and take any short-cuts, your dog will soon accept being on the lead, without trying to pull. Be consistent, reward him at every opportunity and remember to try and make it fun and interesting. Have little chats with him whilst you are walking, to keep his attention on you. Passers-by will think you are a little mad, but if it helps to make heelwork more of a pleasure for you both, does it really matter what strangers think of you?

4

THE AGGRESSIVE DOG

Sadly, some dogs are, or become, aggressive. It is difficult to generalise over possible cures without seeing and assessing each individual case, but I will go into some of the causes and suggest ways to cope.

If you have a dog who likes to bite, be it other dogs, strangers, family members or even yourself, you may possibly have already thought about muzzling him, re-homing him, or even having him put to sleep.

A muzzle, or some other kind of head restraint, may well stop him from biting, but it won't teach him *not* to, nor help you to find out why he wants to bite in the first place. Re-homing him is simply passing on the problem to somebody else, which is hardly very fair to them or to the dog. The last resort, having the dog painlessly destroyed, should only be considered when you have explored every possible avenue available to you.

What makes a dog aggressive? It could be anything from bad treatment in a previous home, accidental mistreatment, or poor basic training, through to poor breeding or medical ailments.

Bad Treatment in a Previous Home
If you have a 'rescued' dog, you may well not have been given the real reason why the dog needed a new home, either by a previous owner or the rescue kennels, even if

they knew the true reason in the first place.

People who mistreat dogs fall into two groups – those who are deliberately cruel or those who are cruel through ignorance. The result however is the same, a dog who is confused, who will use aggression either to protect himself, or to get his own way.

Despite the bad treatment and subsequent confusion, the dog will still feel insecure when he leaves his 'family' and enters a new one. At first he may behave gratefully and, depending on the basic nature of the dog, this period may be very short, or last for ages. Provided that you are consistent in what you will allow him to do and what you will not permit, in a fair and logical way, the dog should settle in with his new family and will know where he stands. However, if his treatment in the previous home was not consistent, or indeed was deliberately cruel, at some stage he will try to test you, in an attempt to establish his position within the new pack.

If, in the past, he has used aggression as a form of self defence against unfair treatment, or to get what he wanted, he may try to continue to use that behaviour with you. Your reaction to any show of aggression from your dog should depend on the circumstances which initially provoked it.

It may be that the dog has learned to steal and guard a 'trophy', hiding under a table or chair. Here you should avoid a confrontational approach. DO NOT be tempted to drag him out – there lies the path to being bitten! Leave the dog alone, vacate the room, shutting the door behind you. Leave him for half an hour, then return, acting calmly and avoiding eye contact with him. He'll probably come to greet you, leaving his 'den' and his trophy. IGNORE the stolen item, make a fuss of the dog and leave the room again, this time letting him follow you – don't call him out, or he'll probably rush back to get the item. Give him a treat, and making sure he doesn't follow you, go back into the room and remove the offending item!

In future, try to prevent that situation happening. If he's stealing things and bolting to a place of safety, then ensure that there is nothing around to steal! If he's just using the 'bolt-holes' to avoid you, or avoid what he thinks is going to be punishment, remove access to these areas – block them up, move furniture, etc.

In milder cases, when the dog may just 'grumble' at you, say, for instance, he doesn't want to be brushed, or dried with a towel, a firm NO and a steady stare at the dog should be enough. He may well have been hurt in the past when being groomed, so it is hardly surprising that he should defend himself. Don't shout or scream at him – that will just make him grumble even more. Assuming he does stop, this is one case when you DON'T tell him he's a good dog – you only reward the dog when he does something good, not for NOT doing something naughty! When the grumbling stops, just speak calmly to the dog, then make him do something, i.e. sit or down, which you can then reward. This will also further support your role as pack leader – insisting that the dog perform some task for you, which you can then praise.

Once you have established the 'trigger' which provokes the dog, you can either ensure that these situations are avoided, or set up a controlled situation, in order to overcome them. It may be a particular noise, person, place or thing which triggers the defensive aggression.

As an example, let's use the case of a dog whose previous owner used to beat him. Suppose the owner also had a motor-bike and consequently wore a crash helmet. The dog therefore has a remembered association between people wearing crash helmets and pain. You may have owned the dog for some time, but during that time the dog has not come into contact with anyone wearing a helmet. Then one day an innocent visitor arrives at your house by motor-bike and enters your home, either wearing or carrying the helmet. Suddenly, your previously placid, friendly dog becomes a snarling, biting maniac. Exit one visitor, hopefully not hurt, but definitely unimpressed! Your next step is to borrow a crash helmet. Start to treat it as an extension of yourself, carrying it around with you, leaving it beside your chair when you sit down. Be very calm and casual about it, not making any direct reference to the helmet as far as the dog is concerned. Once the dog is used to you walking around with the helmet, start wearing it for a few minutes, several times a day. When he accepts that, leave the helmet by the dog's bowl, until he accepts it completely and ignores it.

The next stage is to set up a dummy situation, of a visitor wearing the helmet and arriving at your house. Enlist the help of a member of the family, or a friend whom the dog knows and likes. Make sure the visitor has plenty of dog-type tit-bits in his pocket. Invite the visitor in, sit him down and talk calmly to him and the dog. Provided there has been no sign of aggression from the dog, the visitor is to offer the dog a tit-bit, talking to him very calmly and quietly. He must not make any sudden moves, or try to touch the dog at this stage.

Any mumbling or grumbling from the dog must be ignored. There must not be any unpleasant connection with the visitor as far as the dog is concerned, and if you told him off in this situation, the dog would associate the visitor with your displeasure, resulting in him being even more determined not to make friends. When all has been calm for about ten minutes, the visitor can start to stroke the dog, again offering more tit-bits.

Once the dog is totally at ease with the visitor, tell him to remove the helmet and place it on the floor beside him. Try putting a tit-bit inside the helmet, encouraging the dog to seek it out. Repeat this whole procedure two or three times over a couple of weeks, using different people each time.

What you are showing the dog is that the situation, i.e. a person wearing a helmet, is no longer a threatening one for him and nothing dreadful is going to happen. All the time he is good, he receives affection and reward, in the shape of stroking and tit-bits.

Eventually, people wearing crash helmets will only provoke pleasant associations for the dog – you may even end up with him actively seeking out people wearing helmets. However, that's another problem!

Apply this type of therapy to whatever is provoking the dog into defensive aggressive behaviour. Although it may seem odd not to chastise the dog for showing aggression, in these situations being punished will simply cause the bad behaviour to escalate. Reward all acts of compliance profusely – remember, once again, that the dog will repeat actions that get your attention and learn quickly *not* to repeat actions that get ignored.

Accidental Mistreatment

This could range from you accidentally treading on your dog's foot, to touching the dog where he has an injury of which you were unaware. Such occasions will stick in your dog's mind as an experience which he will not want repeated.

Let's take the instance when you have accidentally trodden on your dog's foot. No doubt you were very sorry, and in spite of the fact that he snapped at you, you forgave him because it was your fault. You probably even gave him a cuddle, in an attempt to appease him. After that first occasion, he becomes more and more edgy whenever you, or indeed anyone, steps near his feet, and either starts flying out to attack, or alternately running away from them, as he associates the proximity of the feet with the discomfort. How do you solve this without being confrontational and without resorting to punishment as a reinforcement to show your dislike of such behaviour?

You will need to set up a situation, whilst you are wearing boots on your legs for protection, and so stopping you from having any reaction to his aggression. You have to show him that he is not always going to be hurt when people step near him. You are also going to have to tolerate him snapping at you, until he realises that (a) he isn't going to be hurt and (b) snapping at you isn't going to stop you stepping near him. Have plenty of tit-bits ready. Have a long line attached to his collar, so that you can stop him running away from you, but do not be tempted to use the line as a form of correction. It is simply there to ensure the dog remains in close proximity.

So, with your feet and legs protected by the boots, start walking slowly towards the dog, a step at a time. As you take each step, speak to him soothingly and provided the dog hasn't either tried to run, or tried to bite, place a tit-bit on the floor by your foot. Stand still on one foot and gently swing your foot around, close to your dog's face. Again, reward for no reaction, ignore any aggressive reaction. Place a tit-bit on your foot, letting him take it in his own time. Stand still right in front of him and scatter tit-bits all around and on your feet. All the time, speak to him gently and lovingly, reinforcing his good behaviour with lots of 'good dog', etc.

Depending on the nature of your dog, and how much discomfort he experienced when you first accidentally trod on him, this desensitising may take only a couple of days, or a couple of weeks. I would suggest that you do it at least twice a day, for ten minutes each time. When he has accepted your feet being close to him without trying either to attack, or run from you, for at least a week, repeat the whole process wearing soft shoes, and end up actually 'stroking' your dog with your feet, liberally rewarding him with tit-bits and cuddles all the time he accepts the situation. Any sign of grumbling must be completely ignored, and all the time he is grumbling, stop the tit-bits and don't talk to him at all.

Eventually, with patience, you will overcome this problem. Like the helmet situation, if your dog develops a phobia about any normal situation, or a particular sound, apply the same type of therapy. Even if the situation appears ridiculous to you, be aware of the dog's feelings and act accordingly. To put the whole thing onto a human basis, it is much like someone getting cross with you if you are terrified of spiders. It doesn't matter how cross they get, or how stupid they think you are, you just can't tolerate spiders, and their anger, or derision, just makes the whole situation even more stressful. That is exactly how the dog feels!

Incorrect Basic Training

Dogs do not naturally know right from wrong. Unfortunately many owners unintentionally allow their dogs to become aggressive, by permitting certain behaviour. This is especially so with young puppies, when signs of aggression are allowed because 'he's only a baby'. It can also happen when you give a home to a rescued dog. You try to compensate him for the trauma he has gone through, by being too soft and feeling sorry for him.

In the same way, dogs who are not given the opportunity to socialise with other people and/or dogs, will often show aggressive tendencies when they do eventually come into contact with people and dogs they do not know.

It is obviously better for all concerned to socialise the dog properly. By socialise, I mean regular interaction with other people, dogs, other animals, places, etc. During these periods of socialising, the dog learns valuable lessons in the correct way to interact with people and dogs, from the reactions *he* receives in response to his behaviour. If he is of a nervous disposition, he will learn that if he runs from another dog, he will probably be chased, whilst if he stays still, no harm will come to him. If he is of a 'pushy' nature, he will most likely be put in his place if he should barge up to another dog.

Introduce the dog properly to the world outside his home. Then he will not feel threatened by other people or dogs. There is often a tendency for under-socialised dogs to be protective towards their owners. Most dogs, once they are secure with those they know well, will assume that strangers are equally trustworthy, unless those strangers show warning signs to the contrary.

Some people, either deliberately or through ignorance, may tease the dog into aggressive behaviour. Children, especially those who have not been taught to respect animals, often end up the victim of their own actions, when a dog retaliates against constant teasing.

Other people may be genuinely afraid of dogs, giving off confusing 'vibes' to the dog, which could cause him to act in an aggressively defensive manner.

You are responsible for your dog's actions, so you must be aware how his behaviour is perceived by others. Even if you know absolutely that he is not going to be aggressive, his behaviour may be sending out the wrong signals, or may be being misinterpreted. If the subject of either the real or perceived aggression has innocently sparked off the behaviour, explain to them (in a reasonable manner of course!) what the action was that initiated the dog's behaviour.

Obviously you will not be rewarding your dog for any displays of aggression, but once the incident is resolved, immediately put the dog in the position of doing something for you, even something as simple as sitting, so that you can reward him for *that* behaviour, showing him which type of behaviour gets rewarded, i.e. being obedient. If he is on the lead at the time, do make sure that you don't put any pressure on the lead.

A tight lead can indicate to the dog that there is something to be on guard against. In the same way, tightening the lead in an attempt to stop him showing aggression in the first place will probably provoke him further, into an aggressive display. It can also make the dog feel safe, as by hanging on to him, you are effectively keeping him out of trouble. The dog then feels that you are protecting him, which encourages aggressive displays, as you are not going to let him get hurt.

With the dog either sitting or lying down at your side, with the lead slack, the dog recognises that you are in control and that there is no need for him to act defensively.

If you have been guilty of continually keeping your dog out of trouble when he exhibits aggressive behaviour, this could lead to him resenting others coming close to you, as you are his protector. The intervention of another person can threaten his security, which results in his being over-protective. He will resent anyone attempting to sit next to you and either through aggression, or persistent attention-seeking behaviour, will try to undermine the other person, until he removes himself.

Human nature being what it is, displays like this are often

misinterpreted as the dog seemingly being devoted to you, which is very good for your ego. Because it appears that the dog wants you all to himself, you are inclined to tolerate the behaviour and, worse, condone it by getting the other person to move away. It is up to you to show the dog that, much as you love him, you will not tolerate such intervention between you and another person.

Sometimes, the dog is allowed to develop possessive feelings towards food, toys, furniture or territory.

It is a popular misconception that it is natural for a dog to growl at anyone who ventures near whilst he is eating his food or chewing on a bone. If the dog is permitted to get away with intimidating behaviour over something as important to him as food, he will almost certainly use aggression to achieve lesser goals.

The method described at the beginning of the book when feeding puppies can be used just as effectively with an adult dog, and you must persist until the dog realises he only gets these things because you let him.

The more confident your approach when taking food or bones from him, the quicker he will respond in an acceptable fashion. Any display of possessiveness should be met with a very firm stare and an almost indignant attitude on your part – along the lines of 'you are joking, don't be so ridiculous' said with a dismissive air. Don't give the food or bone back until the dog is obviously contrite over his actions.

The same method should be used if the dog shows possessive traits with his toys. He must be taught that he owns nothing and only has access to toys, etc., if you say so.

It is most important that you and other members of the family are consistent with permission and denials. For instance, if you do not want the dog to play with slippers, but another member of the family gives him a slipper to play with, this will confuse the dog over what is and is not acceptable behaviour. It will also undermine your authority with the dog, making future confrontations harder to deal with.

This also applies to territory and furniture. Either the dog is allowed on the settee or he is not. Either he is allowed in the bedrooms, or he is not. He must not be allowed by some members of the family, yet corrected for being there by others. He will become very confused by this and a confused dog is potentially an aggressive dog. You *can* train him, for example, that he is only allowed on the furniture when he is invited, but first he has to learn that he is only there because you say he can be.

Don't make the mistake of thinking that if others allow him to have, or do, things which you don't, that he will love them more and you less. A dog is much more secure when he knows exactly where his place is and is also much more secure when he can instantly recognise who is the leader of his 'pack'.

Mouthing and Play-Biting
Last in this category of poor basic training comes the dog who likes to mouth your hand and sometimes other parts of your body and your clothes. If you have a puppy you may well be experiencing this, but those of you with adult dogs may also be having trouble with this, caused through illogical training when the dog was a youngster.

You may have already tried shouting at the dog, or slapping his nose, but these actions can actually make the problem worse, and could indeed actively encourage the dog to attempt to bite, initially in play but eventually getting more serious.

To use the logical approach, remember back to when your dog was in the litter, with his brothers and sisters. By play-fighting, one of the lessons the puppy learns is **bite-inhibition**. When one puppy bites another puppy too hard, the bitten puppy yelps or squeals loudly, sometimes snapping back or sometimes running away. Either way, the game is usually called to a halt, and the 'biter' learns that his actions caused the game to end. Likewise, if **he** gets bitten too hard during the game, he will squeal etc., to let the other puppy know that he is being too rough. The puppies learn, by their littermates' reactions, to modify their biting and to treat each other more gently.

What we as owners should now do is use the same reaction when the puppy or dog goes to place its teeth on you. Scream loudly 'OUCH', or better still, try to yelp like a puppy would. The more dramatic your reaction, the more effect it will have on the dog. Pretend to sulk for a few seconds, in an 'I'm not playing with you if you're going to be so rough' attitude. Then offer your hand back to the dog, saying softly 'gently' – and if the dog nudges or licks your hand, tell him what a clever dog he is. You may need to repeat this a few times, but the dog will learn, as he did with his brothers and sisters, that biting is a no-no.

Do not encourage rough or competitive play with your dog at any time, especially with children. When their play gets too boisterous, this is when the dog can get over-excited and will start to mouth again. It is not that the dog is automatically aggressive – to him it is natural to use his teeth, but unfortunately this can lead to the dog hurting you and in turn ends up with you losing your temper, shouting at the dog and perhaps slapping him, in an attempt to re-gain control. Although seemingly logical to us, the louder and more physical you become, the more the dog gets 'wound up', resulting in him attempting to bite harder, possibly ending up doing serious damage.

Chase type games should always be avoided, as this encourages the dog to jump and bite, either at clothes or hands. Similarly, games with tug type toys should also be avoided. These types of game place the dog in a competitive situation – if he wins the 'trophy' it will reinforce his opinion that he is top dog and will hinder future training. If you win, through brute force, it will make the dog even more determined to use his stronger qualities, i.e. his teeth, in any future confrontation over perceived trophies.

It is instinctive for a dog to try to win in a confrontation – that is how he survived in the wild. What we have to do is to make the 'losing' as pleasant and as non-confrontational as possible. When he tries to chew you or your clothes, give him something he *can* chew, such as a toy. As previously mentioned, try not to get involved in situations where one of you has to physically win. For example, don't be tempted into chasing after the dog if he steals something, as this again will become a win or lose situation. (See also *Dogs who Steal*, page 32.) Encourage him to give up what he has stolen by offering an alternative that he *is* allowed, or better still, in this case offer him food as a reward – food is, after all, his number one priority.

Remember that for a dog to use his teeth to 'hold' things, be it us or our clothes, is all quite natural for the dog and is not wrong – it is simply that it is not acceptable to us and we have to make it clear to the dog that we will neither encourage such behaviour nor allow it to develop.

Being Bitten by Another Dog

If your dog has been intimidated, attacked or bitten by another dog, he may make a point of avoiding that particular dog, dogs of that particular breed, or indeed all dogs. However, it can affect him the other way – he might actively want to attack that dog, breed type or all dogs.

Both these reactions are understandable and naturally you will have great sympathy with the dog's feelings. In the first instance, if you allow him to avoid the dog and over-protect him, you could actually make him more nervous. Of course, if the attacker is a known aggressive dog, not being properly controlled by the owner, it is common sense for you to avoid it and take whatever action you deem appropriate to prevent the situation happening again.

If it was just a one-off incident, over-protection by you will lead to him being even more wary. You will need to help the dog to regain his confidence, without 'babying' him. One of the best places to do this is at a dog training club where they teach modern, NON punishment orientated techniques and where the instructors have the proper experience and qualifications.

Leaving his Natural Mother at the Wrong Age

Sometimes, either through ignorance on the part of the breeder, or circumstances such as the bitch dying, puppies are taken from their natural mother too early. The ideal age for a pup to leave his mum is between seven to nine weeks, which is the crucial man-bonding time. Leaving mum and his litter brothers and sisters before this time means that he misses out on vital parts of his formative education and development.

The bitch teaches her pups what behaviour is acceptable, by admonishing them very firmly when they step out of line. She shows them, by example, how to interact with humans, what to be wary of and what things and situations are harmless.

Leaving his litter brothers and sisters too soon, he will not have completed learning the rules of behaviour when encountering other dogs. By play fighting in the litter, he learns how to moderate his behaviour so as not to cause discomfort, by experiencing early on what over-boisterous behaviour provokes in his litter mates. He learns the correct postures and signals to use when encountering another dog. If this learning is curtailed by leaving the litter before seven weeks old, he will not recognise these signals when he meets his first strange dog and may react in an aggressive fashion. Likewise, because *he* will be giving out confusing signals to the strange dog, that dog may act aggressively, because he is confused by the behaviour he is encountering.

This particularly applies when pups are orphaned at birth and hand-reared by humans. They tend to form a very deep attachment to the person who rears them, which in turn can lead to the pup being very possessive towards people. Not having had the benefit of another canine's teaching in proper dog behaviour, they are inclined to feel antagonistic towards other dogs, and will always relate closer to humans, perhaps finding other dogs a threat to that human relationship.

The reverse can happen if the pup stays with his mum too long, i.e. beyond nine weeks. Because he remains in a dog-oriented environment beyond the man-bonding time, he will relate more easily with dogs than with people, resulting in him being uneasy in human company, which could show itself as either very nervous behaviour or in displays of aggression.

If any of the above applies to your dog, you must pay great attention to socialising him, being scrupulously clear with your correction and reward. It would be very helpful if you could befriend someone who has a docile female dog, as she can help with showing your dog, in canine language, what behaviour is acceptable. Joining a dog training club could well help with finding a suitable companion for this purpose.

You may never achieve complete success in your attempts to mix your dog with other dogs and people, but you should achieve a level at which your dog can co-exist with both.

Poor Breeding

Although the majority of breeders are very selective, there are unfortunately many people who breed from unsuitable stock, often for very dubious reasons.

Some people breed from their bitch in the mistaken belief that it will 'be good for her to have a litter'. Even worse are those who breed from a bitch who has a poor temperament because they think it will improve it. Others breed simply with an eye to making money from the sale of the litter and, worst of all, are the puppy farmers, who over-breed their bitches, without giving a thought either to temperament, or to the health of the bitch or her pups.

Some of these people may well check the bitch and prospective stud dog for genetic faults, but do not give the same attention to the temperament of the prospective parents. Their offspring will inherit character traits from them both. Often the bitch is bred from far too early, without being given the chance to mature properly, either mentally or physically. As already mentioned, a bitch teaches her pups much by example and if she is nervous or immature, she will pass her own fears and phobias on to her offspring.

Inexperienced or ignorant breeders often fail to give correct advice to new owners, when they ask for help, particularly when the owners find the dog showing character traits which they cannot understand. If poor breeding could be the reason why your dog is showing aggressive signs, you will need patience, positive training and the help of a good dog training club, to help you get the best from your dog.

Choosing a Breeder

Whilst on the subject of breeding, if you are reading this book prior to getting your puppy, do make sure that you choose the breeder very carefully. Don't be tempted to buy the puppy which gazes at you appealingly from the nearest pet shop window. Although there are good pet shops, there are also plenty who do not enquire too deeply into the origins of their stock. It is also advisable to avoid the one-off private breeder, who may fall into one of the categories previously mentioned, or at best will not have the expertise needed to raise a litter properly.

The safest way to obtain a puppy is either by personal recommendation, or, once you have decided on the particular breed you want, obtain a list of registered breeders from the Kennel Club.

Before you go and see the puppies, find out about any genetic defects which can occur in your chosen breed. Ask the breeder if both the bitch and the stud dog have been tested for these defects. For some conditions, such as hip dysplasia, there are schemes for submitting the results of such tests to a veterinary panel, who 'award' points depending on the severity of the defect. Ask your local vet to explain the scoring system to you, so that you are fully aware before you go and see the puppies.

Often, the breeder does not own the stud dog, so it may not be possible for you to see him. However, when you do eventually go to see the puppies, make sure you see the bitch as well. If the breeder does not let you see her, *do not buy one of the puppies*. Most breeders are only too happy to let you see their stock, so any reluctance on their part to let you see the mother of the puppy you intend to buy should be viewed with the greatest suspicion.

You should be able to observe the bitch with her pups, when you will have the chance to study her temperament, bearing in mind the important part it plays in the development and character of your chosen pup. It is understandable if she shows some apprehension should you touch her puppies – when you want to start picking them up, the breeder will probably remove her from the room.

If she shows any other displays of nervousness or aggression, please think very carefully before buying one. To see a litter of puppies is a wonderful sight and it is easy to get carried away, letting your heart rule your head and not paying sufficient attention to the character of the bitch. A bad decision at this stage though could mean the beginning of years of trauma and heartache for you and your family.

Assuming that the bitch's temperament is all that it should be and the pups are obviously healthy and well adjusted, you then have to choose one! It is not necessarily a good idea to go for the biggest and boldest pup in the litter. He has become like that by pushing and bullying his brothers and sisters, having found that he gets a bigger share of food and attention that way. Although this need not be a fault, if you do pick this bossy puppy, you must be prepared for him to try that behaviour out on you, so if you are of a gentle and quiet disposition, this pup may not be the right one for you.

In the same way, the quietest pup in the litter will not adapt very easily if you have a noisy home full of boisterous children!

It is very much a matter of personal choice, but do try to use common sense if possible. Personally, I'm a great believer in instinct when it comes to selecting a puppy, but then not everyone's instincts are the right ones!

Medical Ailments

You may have read all the categories previously mentioned, yet still cannot 'fit' your dog into any one of them, so cannot understand *why* your dog is being aggressive.

If this is the case, it would be advisable to have your dog

thoroughly checked over by your veterinary surgeon. Simple things, such as ear infections, bad teeth, blocked anal glands, etc., can cause your dog to be bad tempered. Once treated, you may find that his aggressive behaviour ceases.

Unfortunately, there are more serious conditions, such as brain tumours, which cause the dog to act irrationally. Obviously in such cases, your vet is the best person qualified to give an opinion as to the dog's future.

Dangerous Dogs

The final category which should be mentioned is the dog that has been specifically bred for fighting, and in some instances is actually *encouraged* to be aggressive. Of these dogs, the most notable is the American Pit Bull Terrier. Following a spate of attacks on people by these dogs, and also, it must be said, by some other breeds, the Dangerous Dogs Act 1991 and Dangerous Dogs (Amendment) Act 1997, passed in June 1997, was brought into force. Hopefully, none of the readers of this book will ever find themselves in possession of a truly vicious dog, but it is as well to know the outline of this Act, so on page 126 I give details of it.

5

KEEPING YOUR DOG HEALTHY

With luck, your dog will lead a long and healthy life. A few sensible precautions on your part will increase the chances of your dog doing just that. You also have a responsibility to ensure that your dog does not spread disease to other dogs or indeed to humans.

Regular Inoculations
With the system currently in operation in this country, killer diseases which can affect dogs have been closely controlled and in some cases almost eradicated.

The most lethal of them all, rabies, has been so far excluded from the UK and Ireland by the quarantine laws. Quarantine means long separation from our dogs, which is not very pleasant, but it is infinitely better than bringing in a disease which could have such awful consequences on domestic animals, wild life and humans. At the time of writing, Britain's quarantine laws are under review, and there are suggestions that the current system may be abolished or radically altered. See page 118 for details of the Pet Travel Scheme.

It is up to all of us to act responsibly to ensure that rabies never reaches this country and to report any known instances of quarantine evasion to the authorities immediately.

The four main diseases which can be controlled by regular inoculation are distemper, hepatitis, leptospirosis and parvo virus. This last disease, parvo virus, is relatively new. It particularly affects young puppies and elderly dogs and is quite virulent in some parts of the country.

All dogs must be inoculated against these diseases, to lessen even further the chance of an epidemic. Puppies are usually inoculated at around eight weeks and again at twelve weeks. After that, yearly booster inoculations are essential, so that the dog has continual protection throughout his life. Until puppies have received their second inoculation at twelve weeks, they should not be mixed with other dogs.

Worming

There are two groups of worms which can affect dogs, namely the nematode group and the cestode group. These are more commonly known as roundworms and tapeworms. Signs of worm infestation in the dog are abnormal hunger, diarrhoea, anal itching, poor growth and loss of condition.

The unwormed dog can pass worms to other dogs, via the worm eggs. The eggs are passed by the dog in his faeces. These eggs are then moved around by the wind, rain and on the soles of people's shoes. The eggs can then adhere to passing dogs, sticking to their feet and coat. The dog can then ingest the eggs when licking himself, thus the life cycle of the egg continues, resulting in worm infestation.

It is also possible for these eggs to be ingested by humans, especially children. By touching infested ground, or by stroking a dog who has the worm eggs attached to his coat and then putting their hands in their mouths, people can ingest the eggs. The cycle of the egg is then altered and in rare circumstances can lead to blindness and mental retardation. This disease is called Visceral Larvae Migrans and is caused by the egg of the roundworm Toxocara Canis.

There is also a strain of tapeworm, which, if ingested during its development stage, can affect humans, causing a disease called Hydatidosis, which affects the liver and lungs. Fortunately, cases of this disease are extremely rare.

All this unpleasantness can be avoided if all dog owners abide by the following simple rules:

1. All puppies should be wormed before leaving the breeder, at three weeks and five weeks of age. They should be wormed again twice more by the time they reach 13 weeks. Thereafter they should be regularly wormed every six months throughout their lives.

2. Bitches who are about to be bred from should be wormed prior to mating and again after the puppies are weaned.

3. All faeces should be removed daily from the garden and burned or hygienically disposed of. Always remove any faeces your dog leaves behind when out on exercise.

4. Always wash your hands after handling your dog, before consuming food.

By following these simple procedures, you can be assured that you have taken all possible steps to prevent your dog passing the infection to other dogs or humans.

Fleas

Dog fleas are quite indiscriminate and will infest the clean, healthy dog just as much as the dirty, neglected animal. The flea lives on the dog, sucking blood, and its bites can cause extreme irritation. Some dogs also become allergic to the saliva which is injected into the skin when the flea bites. As well as the irritation caused, fleas are also the intermediate host of the tapeworm.

Fleas can be seen quickly moving over the dog's skin and are particularly partial to the base of the dog's tail and behind its ears. Flea droppings look like specks of grit and are especially visible on the dog's stomach. Fleas like warmth and will lay their eggs in the gap between the carpet and the skirting board, between the floorboards, in the pile of fitted carpets and in the dog's bedding and basket. After the eggs hatch, the larvae stage can remain dormant for anything up to one year, if the temperature is not warm enough.

The adult fleas spend only a short time actually on the dog, just long enough to feed, mate and then they jump off, either onto the floor, another dog or cat, or, worse still, onto you.

At one time, flea infestations were confined to the warmer summer months, but nowadays, with more and more homes being centrally heated, the larvae can hatch all year round, jumping on to the next passing host, after hatching. There are various types of flea prevention preparations available from your vet, and by regular treatment of the dog, and other pets, you should keep this problem at bay. Do remember to treat all pet bedding, the carpet and the car, and any areas where the animal regularly lies, with the proper preparation from your vet. If you only treat the animal, without doing the animal's environment, you will be leaving all the eggs to hatch out and re-infect the animal. Regular use of the vacuum cleaner will also help to keep the home flea free.

Stings

Bee and wasp stings can cause the same reaction in dogs as they can in humans. Unfortunately it is usually the young puppies who are curious about these flying creatures and try to catch them, often ending up swallowing them. Consequently it is usually the mouth, especially the throat area which gets stung. Immediate first-aid treatment can be applied, where possible, by bathing the area with, for a wasp sting, vinegar, and for a bee sting, bicarbonate of soda. You should also seek immediate advice from a vet. If the mouth or throat area has been stung, it may well swell up and block the airway, so don't take chances – call the vet.

Snake Bites

The only poisonous snake living wild in Britain is the adder. They tend to be shy creatures and will try and keep out of the way. Unfortunately, sometimes dogs will come across them in the long grass or even occasionally basking in the sunshine on a country path. If you suspect that your dog has been bitten **get**

him to a vet. Don't allow the dog to run, as this could accelerate the spread of the venom through the dog's system. If possible, carry the dog, trying to keep calm so as not to cause him any distress. Collapse from snake bite can be almost immediate, depending on the size of the dog. A large breed may only show mild distress, but you must still seek veterinary advice.

Diseases Transmittable to Humans from Dogs

Having previously mentioned how the presence of worms in your dog could, in rare instances, affect humans, there are other conditions that can transfer from dogs to humans. One of these is *Sarcoptic Mange*, which is a skin condition caused by a mite which burrows through the skin. In the dog, this results in fur loss and skin irritation, and when it is passed to humans, the mite can cause a transient skin disorder. Although not life-threatening, it can be most unpleasant and will need medical attention. Obviously, the dog will also require veterinary treatment.

RINGWORM. Although the name of this condition suggests it is caused by a worm, it is in fact a fungal infection, similar to athletes's foot, and is contagious to humans. It affects the skin, and is seen as a ring shape, causing the skin to itch and redden and affecting the hair cells. This condition, though unpleasant, is not life-threatening and responds well to treatment.

RABIES. Having previously mentioned the quarantine laws currently in force, it is to be hoped that we never see the effect that this awful virus can have on mankind. The infection is passed from rabid animals (not just dogs) via the animal's saliva, usually through a bite, but occasionally the saliva can be transmitted via a pre-existing skin wound. It then attacks the nervous system and subsequently enters the brain. The condition is invariably fatal in both animals and man.

Exercise

It is impossible to generalise over how much exercise you should give your dog. Some need a five mile walk daily, whilst others only need a short run around the park. As a very rough guide, medium to large breeds such as Alsatians, Retrievers, Labradors, Collies, etc., should have at least one *good* walk every day, supplemented with shorter walks on the lead. The very large heavy breeds, such as Newfoundlands, Pyreneans and St. Bernards, should not be run for miles and miles – they are quite content to have shorter, more sedate regular exercise, although they can walk a fair distance at a gentle pace. With the smaller breeds, it very much depends on the type of dog – some small dogs can run for hours, whilst others can only take exercise in short bursts. Find out from the breeder, or the vet, exactly how much your particular dog should have. With very young puppies, especially those who are going to grow into big dogs, exercise should be very moderate during the first few months, as their young bones are forming all the time and could be damaged through over exercise.

Grooming

Whether your dog has a short or long coat, he should be brushed regularly, to keep his coat healthy, clean and tangle-free. The shorter-coated dog should be brushed at least once a week, whilst the dog with a longer coat needs brushing daily to keep it in tip-top condition. A few minutes spent every day is far better than half an hour once a week. When you are brushing your dog, it is also a good time to check him over and examine him.

Bathing

It is really a personal choice as to how often you bath your dog, but regular brushing should be sufficient most of the time. Obviously, if your dog has rolled in something unpleasant, or during a heavy moult, a bath may be necessary. It is also a good idea to bath a bitch once she has finished her season, to get rid of any 'interesting' smells which may remain. On these occasions, do use a proper, good quality dog shampoo and rinse the coat thoroughly.

Where possible, bath your dog on a warm, sunny day, so that after you have removed the excess water with a towel, your dog can stay outside and dry his coat properly. If it is a cold or wet day, dry as much as possible with a towel, then use a hair drier, or let him lie in front of a warm, but not hot, fire. Make sure that his joints are dried thoroughly, to prevent any future problems with rheumatism.

Swimming

Many dogs enjoy swimming and it can be very good exercise for them. If you do allow your dog into the sea, you must rinse his coat well in fresh water when you return home, as the salt and the sand can cause skin irritation. Also, please be considerate if you take your dog onto the beach. It can be very annoying for other beach users to have a dog running through their possessions and having to avoid the little 'piles' which dogs can leave behind them!

Heat Stroke

Most dogs do not enjoy being exposed to hot sun. Their body temperature is higher than ours and their tolerance of heat is lower. During the summer months, it is best to restrict the dog to light exercise during the heat of the day, leaving strenuous exercise either for early morning or evening. Make sure they always have access to both shade and water.

Never leave a dog unattended in a car during warm weather. Even with the windows open, the temperature can soar within minutes, causing the dog extreme distress, which can lead very quickly to collapse and death. I did an experiment with my own car, to see what the temperature was inside, on a hot, sunny day. The car, an estate, was parked on the roadside, with a small amount of shade being cast on it. The outside temperature was 80° Fahrenheit.

With all the windows fully opened, the sunroof and the

tailgate open, after ten minutes the temperature inside the car was the same as outside, i.e. 80°.

With the windows half open, the sunroof open and the tailgate shut (as you may possibly leave the car when popping into a shop), within ten minutes the temperature inside the car was 98°.

With windows, sunroof and tailgate all shut, the temperature inside the car reached 122° within ten minutes. So, you can see that even with leaving windows opened, the dog would very quickly be overcome by the heat and lack of air circulation.

However, if you ever come across a dog which is unfortunate enough to suffer from heat stroke, you must take action fast. The signs are panting, profuse salivation, vomiting and general weakness. Quickly move the dog to a cool, airy place and apply cold water and/or ice packs to the head, neck and shoulders and seek veterinary assistance immediately.

Feeding

Nowadays, the choice of what to feed your dog is very extensive, ranging from fresh meat, canned meat, all-in-one dried foods, to various forms of processed food. What you decide upon is basically a personal matter between you and your dog, but don't allow him to become a fussy eater. If he turns his nose up at what you provide, don't immediately rush out and buy something different. Assuming he is not ill and provided that the food is not stale, leave the bowl down for a couple of minutes and if he hasn't eaten it, pick it up again. Try him once more, half an hour later and if he still doesn't eat, remove the bowl, keep the food fresh and give it to him for his next meal. Dogs are not stupid. He will not starve himself. He can actually survive for several days without food, provided he has access to fresh water. Obviously, if your dog has previously been a good, unfussy eater and suddenly goes off his food, something is wrong and you should take him to the vet. This is particularly so with young puppies.

All dogs are different – some gulp their food down ravenously, whilst others pick delicately, taking a long time to clear their dishes. However, if you have the type of dog who will only eat best steak, then that's because *you* have let him choose. After all, I'm sure you'd rather eat steak than fish fingers, given the choice, but cost dictates that you can't!

If you decide to feed your dog fresh meat, give it to him raw and don't waste all the essential vitamins by boiling them out during cooking. You may not like the look of raw meat, but I assure you your dog will – and the taste! In the wild, dogs didn't carry their primus stoves around with them to cook their kill on! Their teeth and stomachs are designed for eating and digesting raw meat, so please, don't cook it.

Don't feed him solely on meat and biscuits. Substitute the biscuit with bran occasionally – particularly if your dog is putting on weight when he shouldn't. Bran is a very good filler and will make him feel replete without putting on unwanted weight. Feed him vegetables too, raw if possible.

If you are having temperament problems with your dog, either with aggression, or hyper-activity, have a look at his diet. There has been some research done, which has shown that a reduction in the protein content of the dog's diet can have a calming effect on such dogs, over a period. Basically, too much protein can over-fuel the dog, in the same way as extra oats charge-up a horse. If you feel your dog fits into one of these categories, try changing to a food high in cereals and feed white meat rather than red – in fact choose a blander diet overall.

Once your dog is past puppyhood and is on a balanced diet, there is no need to give him any liquid other than water to drink. Milk is not necessary and can in fact upset the stomach. Too much milk is also a big factor in dogs becoming over-weight.

Don't be tempted to feed your dog 'human' food as tit-bits. Chocolate designed for us to eat is not suitable for your dog. It contains refined sugar, which the dog cannot digest. The fact that he will eat it if offered is quite irrelevant – given the chance he'll eat all kinds of things that aren't good for him.

If you must give your dog tit-bits, either buy a proprietary brand of dog treats, or give him apples or a small piece of cheese. Apples contain natural sugar, which the dog can digest and most dogs love cheese, which does no harm in small quantities.

As regards to the amount you should feed, a rough guide is to feed ½ oz of total food per pound of target bodyweight. For example, if your dog should weigh 30 lbs, then he should have no more than 15 oz of total food per day. Like people, dogs have varying metabolic rates and some dogs may get overweight given the average quantity of food per day. With growing puppies, the diet will obviously not be the same as for a full-grown dog – if you have not obtained a diet sheet from the breeder, get advice from your vet. As dogs grow old, their food requirements may change, so again, get advice from the vet.

Castration

Earlier in the book, I briefly touched on the subject of castrating a male dog and the possible outcome of such action. Apart from the obvious fact that castrated males cannot reproduce, it can, in certain cases, help with behavioural problems. But castration is not the answer to every training problem. It does not stop them forever sniffing the ground, sniffing other dogs or sniffing humans in places that we wish they wouldn't! It will not stop them recognising the difference between male and female dogs and it will not stop them cocking their legs. Neither will it automatically stop them from running off, or attempting to mount bitches.

Having listed the things which castration will probably not help, there are some occasions when it can have positive results. If your dog is very sexually possessive, for example with one particular member of the family, or with a female dog who lives in the same house, and this possessiveness culminates in shows of aggression, then castrating the dog can have beneficial results. It does not work overnight, however, and can take anything up to six months before you see any improvement. You should not rely on the operation to stop the problem on its own and you should train the dog at the same time, preferably with the help of a good training club, so that the combination will produce the required results.

As I mentioned in the opening chapter, injections simulating castration can be tried first, to assess their reaction before taking the step of having your dog operated on.

If you are contemplating having your dog castrated, please wait until he is properly mature. A dog neutered while still a puppy will not develop properly, either physically or mentally. Once you have had him castrated, watch his weight carefully, as the act of castration, which prevents the circulation of the hormone testosterone, can result in an increase of fat, due to a lowered metabolic rate. Any sign of weight increase should be dealt with immediately – too much weight causes numerous health problems and can kill your dog.

Spaying

If you have a female dog, she will come into season roughly twice a year, starting any time after five or six months of age. The term 'season' means that, for three to four weeks at a time, her body will go through the process which, if allowed, will culminate in mating and the production of puppies. I know that some people are of the opinion that it does a bitch good to allow to her to have a litter. I have not seen any evidence to prove this theory.

In my opinion, unless you have an exceptional specimen of a particular breed and know that you can get good homes for all the puppies, to breed from a bitch, just because it's natural, is very irresponsible. Even worse are those people who breed from their bitch to make money from the sale of the puppies. Dog breeding should be left to the knowledge-able specialist. Indeed, if the laws regarding breeding were tightened up and revolting places like puppy farms and dog supermarkets were closed down, we would see a dramatic reduction in the number of unwanted dogs, pedigree and non-pedigree alike, sitting in rescue centres up and down the country.

Before any bitch is bred from, she should firstly be at least two years old and have had tests to see whether she carries any genetic abnormalities, with the chosen stud dog also tested in the same way. It is the responsibility of the breeder to ensure that all puppies go to a good home and they should also be prepared to take back any puppies who cannot be kept by their new owners.

Dog breeding takes planning – it is not just a case of putting any old bitch to the nearest male dog and letting them do what comes naturally.

So, assuming that you are not going to breed from your bitch, you have two choices. You can ensure that each time she comes into season, for the entire length of the season, that she is kept away from all male dogs and only exercised on the lead, well away from all other dogs. Or you could put her into kennels each time she has a season, which could prove very costly.

The alternative is to have her spayed – that is to remove her ovaries surgically and in some cases part of the uterus, thus stopping the seasons and making it impossible for her to reproduce. The operation itself is very common and should ideally be done after the bitch has had her first season, preferably mid-way between the end of the first one and the beginning of the second.

You can have her spayed before she ever has a season, but I would strongly advise against this. Although physically possible, I have seen the mental result of bitches being spayed before they have had a season. Many of them get mentally screwed up at around the time when their season would have been due.

The fact that some vets will perform the operation before the bitch has had one season does not, to me, make it right.

After all, the vet doesn't have to live with the mental effect that it can have on the bitch. I also like to know that my bitch has developed normally, allowing her to go through the process of one season first, before being spayed.

Passports for Pets

A pilot Pet Travel Scheme (PETS), also known as Passports for Pets, was introduced in 2001. Although currently not available in all countries, where it is in operation certain stringent conditions have to be adhered to *before* your pet can travel – including having the dog micro-chipped, having him vaccinated against rabies, followed by blood tests, and also being properly treated for ticks and fleas. Full details of all the legal requirements can be obtained from your vet.

6

INTRODUCING A SECOND DOG

Nowadays, many families are becoming multi-dog. They start with one, then get another as company for the first one and so on. Normally, second and subsequent dogs join the family without any problems, but there are things which you can do to aid the acceptance process.

Generally speaking, if you already have a male dog, it is better to choose a female as the second dog. There is less risk of fighting between male and female, whereas male dogs can be very territorial and resent another male dog intruding on their territory. Naturally, care must be taken with a male and female dog in the same household when the bitch comes into season, but having her spayed after the first season will resolve that problem. There *is* a slight possibility that once your male dog has a female dog for a companion, he may become a little possessive towards her, by showing aggression to other male dogs who approach his bitch.

Whichever sex you decide upon, try and arrange for their first meeting to be on neutral territory, in case the first dog should show any territorial aggression towards the newcomer. Obviously, if the new dog is a young puppy, you will have to bring the pup straight home, but make sure that the first dog's favourite and most loved member of the family is not the one who carries the puppy indoors. Usually, whatever sex the new puppy is, the original dog will make allowances, and will recognise it as a baby, who offers no threat to his position within the family.

Whether it's a puppy or an older dog, both dogs will adjust more easily if you accept that between them, *they* will work out who is going to be boss dog over the other. Don't try and use human logic by assuming that the dog who was in the house first should be number one dog. It may turn out that way, but if it doesn't and you interfere and upset the natural order of things, you could end up with a very unpleasant situation. By watching their behaviour towards one another, you will quickly see which dog is showing signs of subservience. The underdog will possibly lie down when the other approaches and sniffs him. He may allow the other dog to take his food – here you *should* interfere, by feeding the two dogs separately, or you will end up with one very overweight dog! Boss dog will demonstrate his superiority by pushing the other out of the way when affection is in the offing. He will always try to be the first out of the door when going for walks and first into the car when going for a ride. He may well threaten the other dog verbally, to instil his dominance.

Don't try to treat the two dogs as equals – in their world equality does not exist, remember their basic instincts. Once the pecking order has been established, don't be tempted to compensate the underdog by cuddling him more than the boss dog, or feeding him an extra tit-bit. This will merely antagonise the boss dog, who will then punish his subordinate for what he considers to be liberty-taking and getting above his position.

Always allow boss dog to be first through the door, after you. Feed him first, welcome him first when you come in. You are not showing favouritism by doing this – you're simply accepting the natural order which both dogs recognise.

If you have an elderly dog and are bringing a young puppy into the household, you must obviously take care that the boisterous behaviour of the youngster does not harm the old dog. The youngster will obviously want to play and here you can shield the older dog a little, by getting on to the floor and playing with the pup yourself, to deflect unwanted attention away from the older one. Having said that, don't interfere when the older dog tells the puppy off. He must be allowed to put the pup in his place, or the youngster could make the older dog's life a misery.

Very often, you find that bringing a young puppy into the household can revitalise the older dog, so don't worry too much, just be sensible.

Whilst on the subject of having second and subsequent dogs, please don't be tempted to get two puppies together, as this can have disastrous consequences. I have a friend who says that 'puppy plus puppy equals puppy squared' and it will certainly feel like that at times – two puppies together can wreak the havoc of four!

Firstly, the puppies will always relate to one another, before you, especially if they are litter brothers or sisters, as they will have been together since birth. Two puppies living together will form an attachment that is far more important to them than any human attachment. They will gang-up, as together they are a pack. Because they are a pack, they may become aggressive to other, single dogs.

If one is a chewer, he will influence the non-chewer, not the other way around. They will compete with one another at every opportunity. Walking on the lead will turn into a race, as will getting out of the front door, getting to their food, etc. If one is a barker, he will encourage the other to bark. Having two together will lead you to lump them together, rather than letting their individual characters emerge. When it comes to house training, the slower of the two to become clean will influence the other into being dirty again.

I could cite many more examples of why having two puppies together could be a dreadful combination. If you feel that I am coming strong on this subject, it is because many years ago, I did exactly what I'm trying to deter you from doing. I obtained two dear little cross-bred puppies – I just couldn't separate them – and the ensuing round of catastrophies led me to joining a dog training club and getting hooked on dog training! I would add that both dogs lived to a grand age, but not before they had made a good job of trying to wreck each other, my home and my nerves! Since then, I have met many people who have made the same mistake and were pulling their hair out over the antics of their puppies. So, if it is your intention to go and get two puppies, please think again. Get one first, let him reach maturity, then go and get the second.

Full Circle
So, you've just brought your second dog home. Turn back to the beginning of the book . . .

INDEX

The Dangerous Dogs Act 1991

The Act states that any dog of the type known as the Pit Bull Terrier, any dog of the type known as the Japanese Tosa, and any dog being of a type appearing to have been bred for fighting, *must*:

Not be bred from.
Not be sold, exchanged, advertised for sale or given as a gift.
Not be abandoned, or allowed to stray.
When in a public place be muzzled and held on a lead.
Be securely held by a person over sixteen years of age.

Penalties for disobeying the above may include any or all of the following:

The dog would be destroyed.
The owner would be liable for a fine, or a term of imprisonment, or both.
The owner may be disqualified from keeping a dog, for such a period as the court deems fit.

The Act can also be enforced against *any* breed of dog which is deemed to be dangerously out of control in a public place. Even if the dog has not injured anyone, if there are grounds for reasonable apprehension that it may do so, the Act allows for all or any of the restrictions to be enforced.

There are some dogs, bred from 'fighting' stock, but owned by responsible people, who keep the dog simply as a pet and never allow it to develop aggressive tendencies. It is most unfortunate that these owners are penalized, because of the actions of others. However, as the Act stands, all owners of the breeds mentioned must comply with its rules. Likewise, *all* dog owners must be diligent and act responsibly, to ensure that the actions of their dogs are not misunderstood or misinterpreted.

RIGHT WAY
PUBLISHING POLICY

HOW WE SELECT TITLES

RIGHT WAY consider carefully every deserving manuscript. Where an author is an authority on his subject but an inexperienced writer, we provide first-class editorial help. The standards we set make sure that every **RIGHT WAY** book is practical, easy to understand, concise, informative and delightful to read. Our specialist artists are skilled at creating simple illustrations which augment the text wherever necessary.

CONSISTENT QUALITY

At every reprint our books are updated where appropriate, giving our authors the opportunity to include new information.

FAST DELIVERY

We sell **RIGHT WAY** books to the best bookshops throughout the world. It may be that your bookseller has run out of stock of a particular title. If so, he can order more from us at any time – we have a fine reputation for "same day" despatch, and we supply any order, however small (even a single copy), to any bookseller who has an account with us. We prefer you to buy from your bookseller, as this reminds him of the strong underlying public demand for **RIGHT WAY** books. Readers who live in remote places, or who are housebound, or whose local bookseller is uncooperative, can order direct from us by post.

FREE

If you would like an up-to-date list of all **RIGHT WAY** titles currently available, please send a stamped self-addressed envelope to
ELLIOT RIGHT WAY BOOKS, BRIGHTON ROAD,
LOWER KINGSWOOD, TADWORTH, SURREY, KT20 6TD, U.K.
or visit our web site at www.right-way.co.uk